VISIONARY ROAD

TO THE

CAPITAL

The Little Known Story of John Harris, Jr.

DAVID BISER

Paperback ISBN 978-1-960007-30-8
eBook ISBN 978-1-960007-31-5

Published by

Orison Publishers, Inc.

PO Box 188

Grantham, PA 17027

www.OrisonPublishers.com

The Little Known Story of John Harris, Jr.
October 1727–July 28, 1791

CONTENTS

FOREWORD

There are names from America's founding that every American knows. Many of these even have international reputations. Washington, Jefferson, Franklin, Adams—these names reverberate through our creation story and our culture.

History is often recalled through the lens of these great men, but the truth and reality is that great men do not complete great deeds alone. History is made by people. Great and small, rich and poor, influential or perhaps not. Every one of them had a role on the stage.

Some of the most intriguing of these are what historian Robert K. Brock refers to as wheelhorses—men important to driving the causes forward, sometimes to strong recognition in their own times, but who have not been embraced by the romancing of the past.

In this book, my friend Dave Biser shares with us his research on just such a man. John Harris Jr. is one of these wheelhorses, working to see the founding of a new country, a new government, and a new capital city for Pennsylvania. Harris worked alongside some of the great well-known names—statesmen, important leaders, talented woodsmen, and influential Native Americans.

Dave, however, never loses sight of the fact that John Harris Jr., like any of us, is first a human. Woven throughout his narrative are reminders of the importance of family, the hazards of a life on the edge of civilization, the heartbreak of loss.

Join Dave as he shares his passion of the last fifteen years and enter the world of Harrisburg's founding father.

Ron Carnegie
Costumed interpreter of George Washington
at Colonial Williamsburg, Williamsburg, Virginia

PREFACE

It's been almost fifteen years since I was first asked to walk around at a fund-raising event and pretend to be John Harris Jr., the founder of the city of Harrisburg, Pennsylvania. At the end of that event, I was asked if I would be willing to return for other upcoming events. I politely declined. When asked, "Why not?" I stated that I was interested in an historic portrayal, not in theater or playing dress-up. I let them know that if they were interested in someone doing a first-person portrayal of John Harris, I would be interested, but other than that, no thank you. I got a call from the director of the Historical Society of Dauphin County (HSDC) the very next day. She said she had spoken with several people on the board of directors, and they were impressed with me and wanted to pursue the idea of a first-person interpretation of the founder.

At that point, a bit in a state of shock, I found myself sitting in front of a table laden with all of the data and original works the HSDC owned concerning John Harris. Over the course of the next few weeks, I would spend in excess of thirty hours combing through the material laid out in front of me. I collected important information that I believed would be valuable in telling John Harris Jr.'s story. I learned about his family and work, his faith and values, his connections, his fears, loves, and so much more. And yet somehow, I knew I had just scratched the surface. My next stop was the Pennsylvania State Archives, where a collection of John Harris Jr. data and materials are held for safekeeping. I would spend untold hours handling his original journals and logbooks. Once again, I found significant pieces of history that would make for a powerful, exciting, and interesting presentation.

I have to admit, I was becoming fascinated with the person I was researching. John Harris Jr. was coming to life for me, one fact at a time. The man I was uncovering was impressive, to say the least. Understand, I know of no familial connection to John Harris or to Harrisburg (previously called Harris' Ferry). I have ancestors who would have known of John Harris Jr. and some who may have crossed the Susquehanna River on one of his ferryboats, but I am not a blood relative of Harris. I have done extensive research on my own family, tracing my roots back through the founding of America and across the Atlantic to places like Ireland, Scotland, and Germany. Some of my first American relatives arrived in America via the port in Philadelphia, took the oath of allegiance to the British Crown, and ventured west. Others would eventually settle in Maryland, having crossed the Susquehanna and traveled south. In my adventurous mind, I like to think that there was a day when my family members rolled onto the ferry at Harris's crossing to take the next part of their journey into the unknown future that lay before them. And maybe Harris was there that day and helped them board…. It's just a dream I have.

So, with this new fascination for a person who lived life to its fullest, I began a more in-depth study of who he was and what kinds of things he accomplished. The study and research of a person who lived almost three hundred years ago is not easy. Most individuals who lived back then did not write down everything they did or keep extensive journals of their daily lives. We are fortunate, though, to have sufficient writings by or about John Harris Jr. that we can piece together most of his life. Finding those documents was not easy, and often I discovered new aspects of his life purely by accident.

Unlike George Washington, Benjamin Franklin, or John Hancock, Harris Jr. is a relatively unknown figure in American—and even Pennsylvanian—history. Much of my research was reading what his contemporaries said about him—people such as the governors and lieutenant governors of Pennsylvania, Native American tribal chiefs, other traders like Harris Jr., or even military personnel who came in contact with him.

Details of the life of John Harris Jr. can be found in many places but have never been compiled in one volume. It is my hope that I will do justice to this son, brother, uncle, husband, father, grandfather, pioneer, politician, trader, friend, ferry and tavern owner/operator, brewer, farmer, entrepreneur, and patriot. Those descriptors are the tip of the expansive picture that emerges of this individual, who funded and supported the cause for independence, developed Dauphin County, established Harrisburg, and dreamed that one day, the state capital of Pennsylvania would be on his donated land. When he died in 1791 at the age of sixty-five, his obituary in the August 4, 1791, edition of the Philadelphia *Freeman's Journal* said this:

> *Died, on Friday last, after a short illness, Mr. John Harris, proprietor of this Borough, and on Sunday his remains was deposited in the burying ground of Paxtang Church, being attended by the largest concourse of people ever known here on the like occasion—to whom an excellent funeral sermon was delivered by the Rev. Dr. John Ewing, Provost of the University of Pennsylvania, who happened to be present.*
>
> *Mr. Harris was aged about 65 years and is allowed to have been the first white man born on this side of the Susquehanna, where he resided all his life, without experiencing a day's sickness, except with the small-pox or measles, until that of which he died.*
>
> *He was charitable to the poor, compassionate to the afflicted, and lenitive to those over whom he had power. As a citizen, he was active, and useful; as a husband, parent and master, he was tender, kind and indulgent: beloved in his lifetime by*

most, lamented in his death by all. And such was his desire to promote the instruction of the rising generation in the rudiments of the English and the learned languages, that he made a donation of his ferry over the Susquehanna, for the support of an Academy to be erected at Harrisburgh, and had enjoined in his executors to apply to the legislature of the state for their concurrence and assistance to carry his benevolent designs into execution; and in case of their success, has added several other pecuniary bequests.

—*Freeman's Journal,* August 4, 1791

Most of us would do well to have such wonderful things said about us. For those talking about John Harris Jr., it seemed to come easy. In all my research, I found only one negative comment about him: that he was overly cautious in light of an impending attack on the settlement of Harris' Ferry. John Harris Jr. is among those people whose names are deeply connected to central Pennsylvania, yet few people know his story. I have endeavored to correct this by telling all that I have discovered.

This book is by no means exhaustive, but it covers his entire lifetime, describing not only the moments that make him a hero in our eyes but also the moments that cause us to give him a sideways glance of shame and maybe disgust. Harris Jr. lived in an era when institutions existed that we have long since abolished. We can look back and see the gigantic strides Harris Jr. made, but we must also recognize that he was a flawed human being, like the rest of us, and susceptible to the social ills of his age.

I will tell the story of John Harris Jr. in a more narrative than biographical way. As the sole first-person interpreter of Harris Jr., I have presented him in a format called "in character" by those who perform first-person interpretations. I have studied with and worked alongside members of the Association for Living History, Farm and Agricultural Museums, who present people with last names like Jefferson, Washington, Franklin, Withe, Croghan, and Weiser. John Harris Jr. was a very real person, and to reduce him to a list of bulleted dates and events would be to cancel out the humanity of a person who lived and breathed and felt like all of us do today. So, in an effort to reveal and present the life and times of John Harris Jr., it is important to speak about him as I have come to know and present him. So, here we go.

A FAMILY TREE

John Harris Sr. and Esther Say

Elizabeth (b. 1720–d. 1769) m. John Findley, six children

Esther (b. 1724–d. 1768) m. Dr. William Plunket, four children

John (b. 1727–d. 1791) m. Elizabeth McClure, five children; m. Mary Reed, ten children

William-Augustus (b. 1730–d. 1760) m. Margaret Simpson, two children

Samuel (b. 1733–d. 1825) m. Elizabeth, four children

David (b. 1737–d. ?) m. Miss Mahon, one child

John Harris Jr. and Elizabeth McClure (b. 1729–d. January 20, 1764)

Mary (b. April 13, 1750–d. April 20, 1809) m. William McClay of Paxton (b.1737–d. 1804), nine children

John (b. August 20, 1751–d. 1807) never married

David (b. February 24, 1754–d. November 16, 1809) m. Sarah Crocket, four children

William (b. January 23, 1756–d. July 3, 1764)

Elizabeth (b. November 22, 1759–d. not long after)

John Harris Jr. and Mary Reed (b. 1730–d. November 1, 1787)
Adam (b. November 7, 1765–d. not long after)
James (b. February 15, 1767–d. not long after)
Robert (b. September 5, 1768–d. September 3, 1851) m. Elizabeth
    Ewing, eight children
Mary (b. October 1, 1770–d. August 20, 1851) m. John Andre
    Hanna
Jean (b. March 18, 1772–d. not long after)
Joseph (b. October 23, 1774–d. not long after)
William (b. September 1, 1776–d. August 17, 1777)
Read (b. October 1780–d. not long after)
Elizabeth (b. October 1780–d. not long after)
James (b. 1782–d. May 17, 1806)

Chapter 1

THE STAGE SET
BY JOHN HARRIS SR.

A s best we can tell, John Harris Jr. was born on October 22, 1727, on the frontier of "Penn's Woods" or what we now know as Pennsylvania. His father, John Harris Sr., was said to have immigrated from Yorkshire, England, with just sixteen shillings in his pocket—possibly after seeing a newspaper advertisement placed by William Penn, governor of the Pennsylvania colony. Penn was looking for people to settle the frontier and had placed advertisements in newspapers all over, including in England.

Initially, Harris Sr. labored on the roads and streets of Philadelphia and became a friend of the mayor, Edward Shippen, whom he met in Philadelphia. This connection provided occasion for him to be introduced to Esther Say, Shippen's niece, whom he would marry at Christ Church in Philadelphia. It also gave Harris Sr. an audience with Governor Penn. In 1705, Harris Sr. received a license to trade with Native Americans, settle the land, open a tavern, and operate a ferry across the Susquehanna River. Officially, Harris Sr.—a brewer and all-around handyman—is said to have settled the land that is now Harrisburg in 1717. But it is understood by most that he had likely been scouting the area for at least a year or two prior to 1717.

By watching the movement of the Native Americans, Harris Sr. eventually discovered the reliable and advantageous crossing place where hundreds—maybe thousands—of Native Americans would gather to cross the mighty Susquehanna River during seasons of trade or war with neighboring tribes. And in the pattern of countless other White settlers and frontiersmen during the slow western push, he settled down, building a log cabin, setting up a tavern, establishing a ferry that would take people across the Susquehanna, and beginning a family. It was well known that Penn himself was personally invested in the establishment of a second city in the colony of Pennsylvania—a city that would be second only to rival Philadelphia in beauty and vibrancy. (And while it is often suggested that Pittsburgh is the second city of Pennsylvania, there is little there that can match the beauty of Harrisburg.)

Penn had chosen the Susquehanna River for this new city, and he was in search of strong, well-minded Englishmen who would be willing to set up homesteads on the eastern shore of the river. Harris Sr.'s trading license charged him with erecting "such buildings as are necessary for his trade, and to enclose and improve such quantities of land he shall see fit."[1]

He finally received his warrant in January 1725, which securely granted him five hundred acres. It would serve him well and would be passed on to Harris Jr. when he died in 1748.

In those days, the oldest son inherited everything. So, when Harris Sr. died, John Jr. came into just over eight hundred acres in Paxton, Pennsylvania; as well as multiple buildings; a licensed ferry business, chartered on December 17, 1733, and including an additional three hundred acres; and the responsibility for caring for his three younger siblings, all boys under eighteen years of age.

His two older sisters had married and were out of the house. Elizabeth, the oldest, was married to John Findley and lived nearby. She died young—at forty-nine years of age—in 1769. She bore six children,

---

1 Brown, Carlyle C. *History of John Harris, Founder of Harrisburg, PA.*

who were John's nieces and nephews. John Jr.'s next-oldest sister was Esther Harris, who married Dr. William Plunket of Ireland. He practiced medicine in Carlisle, Pennsylvania; served in the Provincial Army during the French and Indian War; and fought in the American Revolution as a patriot. Esther Plunket died young, like her sister, at the age of forty-six in 1768. She had four children.

John Harris Jr. had lost his father (1748), his mother (1757), and his two older sisters by the time he was forty-two years old. While we know that he was born on the frontier of Pennsylvania, we know little of his upbringing. He was baptized at Christ Church in Philadelphia on September 22, 1728, at the age of eleven months. And while Harris Jr. never wrote about his birthday, researchers like me tend to hold fast to the date of October 22, 1727. It is presumed that he was formally educated in Philadelphia for the most part, due to his parents' connection with that city. But as of yet, no proof of that has been found.

Living on the frontier meant learning the necessities of survival. As a child, young John would have been taught all of the skills needed for working on the farm. This would include managing the seasonal aspects of plantation life, raising livestock, planting and harvesting, seasonal animal slaughtering, fence repair, harvesting trees for firewood, hunting and fishing, gathering nuts and berries, and learning what was okay to eat and what to stay away from. He would have enjoyed life like any child—running through the fields with his brothers and the family dogs, swimming in the river, riding horses bareback, maybe teasing his older sisters, and of course, tending to his studies.

We can easily surmise by the skill of his handwriting, his excellent use of language, the advanced math skills evidenced in his ledger books, and his knowledge of government and politics, that John was well educated and knowledgeable in many areas of life and industry. Being the oldest son, he was more than likely taught the ins and outs of the farm, the ferry business, the tavern, and the trading business by the time he was in his late teens.

His father was still alive in May 1748, when the Provincial Council made John Harris Jr. an ensign in the Provincial Army.

The rank of ensign was the lowest of the officer ranks in the army. By August of that year, he had attained the rank of captain. In December 1748, his father died. While we don't know the cause of Harris Sr.'s death, we know its effect. It left Harris Jr. in charge at the age of twenty-one. He was going to grow up and grow up fast.

John Jr. had three younger brothers to tend to: William-Augustus, eighteen years old (born in 1730); Samuel, fifteen years old (born in 1733), and David, ten years old (born in 1737). John was now the owner of a chartered business that included a license to operate a ferry across the Susquehanna, a license to operate a tavern, a license to trade with Native Americans, over eight hundred acres, multiple buildings and all their holdings, and four Black servants. What an incredible load to place onto the back of a twenty-one-year-old!

Due to the social and legal rules of the time period, John was now the head of the household. Everything that his father owned now belonged to him, and he was empowered to make all of the vital daily decisions that the house and land required. It is good to point out here that those rules would put John's mother, Esther, in an odd and maybe even inconvenient position. Women in the eighteenth century did not have much in the way of power or position. It was rare for a woman to be legitimately independent. Esther was now subject to the decisions made by her eldest son. We know that Esther would marry William McChesney soon after the death of John Sr.—a marriage of which John Jr. did not approve. John attests in his account book that he and his mother had become estranged. We are left to assume that Esther did not feel comfortable staying in the house. She would have known that John would be looking for a wife, and perhaps she thought it would be challenging for two women to run the household. Sadly, she would die in 1757 without repairing the breach in their relationship. She is buried in the Silver Springs Church graveyard in Mechanicsburg, Pennsylvania.

One of the first things Harris Jr. did in 1749, the year following his father's death and his inheritance of the family fortune, was to marry Elizabeth McClure. The Rev. John Elder of Paxton Presbyterian Church performed the wedding. The Harrises would remain faithful members of that congregation for the rest of their lives.

McClure was born in Paxtang in 1729, making her two years younger than John. Raised in the same community, Elizabeth would have known the same people John knew. She would have sat in church and noticed John's presence there. Maybe they "made eyes" at each other. As John had to do as a young man, Elizabeth would have honed all of the skills a young woman would need to survive on the frontier. She was a strong and confident woman—she had to be.

Women built and banked the fires and chopped the firewood for cooking and heating the house. Elizabeth would have learned how to cook and sew and keep a home, most likely a log house. She would have known long days of planting and harvesting, feeding and milking, and she may have known how to fish or shoot a gun. She would have helped "put up" seasonal fruits and vegetables in a way that preserved them long after the growing season ended. She would have been present and expected to help on butchering days.

Her parents would have taught her to keep her eyes open and to always be aware of her surroundings. Not only were there wild animals to contend with, but Paxton occupied a pivotal place on the well-worn north–south trail used by various tribes, such as the Iroquois, Shawnee, Oneida, and Onondaga, on their seasonal treks to visit, negotiate with, or attack other tribes. Elizabeth almost certainly had encounters with them. Prior to the French and Indian War, many encounters between White settlers and people native to the area were civil and friendly. All of that would change in the years following 1753.

Stories about Elizabeth's married life include her quick thinking when a Native American got through the stockade and thrust his rifle through one of the portholes of the house in what may very well have been an attempt to kill a British officer who was visiting Harris Jr. When the rifle failed to discharge, experiencing what is known as a "flash in the pan," Elizabeth quickly blew out the candles in the room to prevent a second attempt. The man ran off, not to be found.

At another time, it is said that an indentured servant who was sent above stairs to fetch something returned without her lit candle. Mrs. Harris calmly went upstairs to find the candle mistakenly resting on a barrel of gun powder. She carefully removed the candle and gave reproof to the young, Irish girl, who most likely had never had the need to know that there was *never* an occasion in which you placed a lit candle on top of a barrel of gunpowder!

John Harris Jr. and Elizabeth had five children, each of them born in the frontier house on the Susquehanna River. Their firstborn was a girl. Mary came into the world on April 13, 1750, just one year after their marriage. This daughter would go on to become the wife of William McClay. Next, John (or Johnny or John III) was born on August 20, 1751. John joined the Continental Army at the beginning of the Revolutionary War. He was possibly wounded at the Battle of Quebec in 1775, when the attacking Continental Army was discovered by British forces and was devastated by canon fire. There is a report that a man named John Harris was wounded at the Battle of Paoli in 1778. According to Harris Jr.'s last will and testament, Johnny was left unable to care for himself due to his wounds. Funds were set aside for his perpetual care after Harris Jr. departed this world.

David, the third child of John and Elizabeth, was born on February 24, 1754. He received a commission in the Pennsylvania Line and became the paymaster for Thompson's Battalion of Riflemen with the rank of major. He would reside in Baltimore, where he died in 1809. A third son, William, was born on January 23, 1756, and died on July 3, 1764, of unrecorded causes. A daughter was born on November 22, 1759, but did not survive.

Harris Jr.'s first love, Elizabeth, died in January 1764 at their home. Her cause of death is, to date, unknown. If the reader needs proof that life on the frontier was difficult and challenging, simply put together the dates of the above-mentioned deaths of Harris Jr.'s loved ones: a daughter in '59, his wife in January of '64, a son in July of '64, a sister in '68, and a sister in '69. It was during these years that the French and Indian War erupted in the British colonies. This conflict wreaked havoc on the frontier of Pennsylvania, and the Harris family was fully involved.

Prior to the war, in 1753, Harris Jr. was commissioned to travel to Logstown, just north of the confluence of the three rivers in western Pennsylvania. His task was to survey and record the trip and to log the mileage from point to point and report his findings to the Pennsylvania government. In the early 1700s, Logstown was a Native American town of approximately two thousand people. Harris Jr. was sent on this trip by the Provincial Congress. It is possible that his secret task was to reconnoiter the situation at Logstown, where it was known that French traders and officers were attempting to win the tribes' allegiance to the French side.

There was third-party news from an unnamed historian that upon his return, Harris Jr. ran into a party of Virginia soldiers and their guides. Harris Jr. knew at least two of the guides who had been hired by the leader of the Virginia party, a man who had been sent to discover the whereabouts and activity of the French on the frontier. George Croghan and Chief Tanaghrisson, otherwise known as Half-King, were hired by Lt. Col. George Washington to guide him and his men into the Pennsylvania wilderness. It was on this trip that the events that sparked the French and Indian War took place.

Harris Jr. would later learn that he had been in the company of Mr. Washington. In October of that same year, Half-King and several of his family members came to Harris' Ferry in a state of great sickness. While there, Half-King succumbed to his illness and died. Harris Jr. petitioned the Pennsylvania government to reimburse him for the funeral expenses of Half-King, which totaled ten pounds fifteen shillings and fourpence. Harris Jr. charged an additional five pounds for his trouble—he was a businessman and an entrepreneur, after all.

But truth be told, Harris Jr. had just lost a friend and an instrumental partner in the work of trading with Native American tribes. It was chiefs like Half-King who placed their trust in Harris Jr. as a White settler. By trust, I do not mean that they trusted him to give them a good deal. While that was a part of the big picture on the Pennsylvania frontier, they also trusted that Harris Jr. knew and cared about them and not just his business or the colonial settlement his father began.

Harris Jr. knew that his colonial Pennsylvania license to trade with Native Americans meant he needed to stay on good terms with the many different tribes in the colony. He also knew that his life and the lives of the many settlers on the frontier depended on a trust between the native people and the White settlers. This trust was fragile, on occasion. There were times when the tribes argued among themselves, and the White settlers became collateral damage as tribes fought one another.

Harris Jr. was familiar with a large number of tribes that lived near Harris' Ferry on the Susquehanna. They included: Seneca, Shawnese (Shawnee), Oneida, Iroquois Nations, Delaware, Leni-Lenape, Tuscarora, Cherokee, Onondaga, and those who made up the Mingos, a western Pennsylvania tribe that was part of the Iroquois confederation. Many of these tribes used the shallow, flat section of the riverbed right in front of Harris Jr.'s house to walk across the almost mile-wide Susquehanna. It was this crossing place that first drew John Harris Sr. to the location that would become his homestead, trading post, and tavern. Archaeological evidence of the Native American presence was identified in a small dig performed in 2022. Pointed stone pieces and fishing tools were found, along with an eighteenth-century French flint.

As a young boy, Harris Jr. witnessed the establishment of the Paxton Presbyterian Church on what is now Progress Avenue in Harrisburg. This land was part of a ridge that formed a natural boundary for the Paxton Valley. The Reverend Elder arrived in Paxton in 1738 to be ordained by the congregation. Prior to Elder's arrival, the people shared a pastor with the congregation at Derry Presbyterian Church. In 1740, when the log building became too small to hold the growing population of Paxton, the hearty settlers undertook a building program. It took several years to complete the new church, since no one was interested in going into debt. Church records tell us that the building was made of local gray stone, much of which came from John Harris Sr.[2] His son would surely have been a part of the hard work of collecting, delivering, and unloading all of those stones.

---

2 Marian Inglewood, *Then and Now in Harrisburg*, (Harrisburg, Pennsylvania, 1925).

Harris Jr. would make the Paxton Church his home congregation, even though he had been baptized an Anglican at Christ Church in Philadelphia. Learning a strong attachment to the church from his parents, he would be married by the pastors of the church and eventually laid to rest in its cemetery, just a few miles from the plantation on the river.[3]

---

3 *Commemorative Biographical Encyclopedia of Dauphin County, Pennsylvania,* Chapter 7, "The Family of the Founder of Harrisburg." (Chambersburg, Pennsylvania: J.M. Runk & Co., 1896), 77.

Chapter 2

FROM CHILD
TO YOUNG ADULT

John Harris Jr. grew up on what would become known as the Harris plantation. Unlike the picture of plantations we have from the Southern colonies, a plantation on the Pennsylvania frontier was more like what we know as a large farm. Like most of us as we grew up, he surely played outdoor games with his two older sisters and three younger brothers. The days would be filled with chores, interacting with the servants who lived on the plantation, fishing in the creeks and the Susquehanna, hunting, and the occasional conversation with Native Americans at his father's trading post.

The younger Harris would spend time in Philadelphia when his father and mother visited with family and cared for trade from the frontier. He would see the day when his father received the license for the tavern, the permission to trade with the natives, and three hundred acres of land. Some historians think John was educated in Philadelphia in an effort to give him the kind of education that was worthy of the son who would one day inherit the entire Harris fortune. As of the writing of this book, we do not have a record of where in Philadelphia he went to receive this kind of education. There were plenty of teachers/tutors in the city in those days. Most likely, he would have gone to someone the family knew or with whom they had some kind of connection. There is a suggestion that his mother, Esther, probably used her family leverage to assure that John got a quality education, since she was a member of the prominent Shippen family. No matter what the actual situation, based on Harris Jr.'s correspondence, we know that he was extremely accomplished at writing and had an extensive vocabulary.

It goes without saying that part of young Harris's education included trips to Philadelphia. These trips would take two to three days, depending on the weather and the number of trade conversations Harris Sr. had in towns like Lancaster or Reading. As a child, Harris Jr. would have met people with whom he would develop adult relationships later on. Men like Conrad Weiser and George Croghan would become lifelong friends. He would meet Native Americans who would also become trusted friends, all because of his father's license to trade.

Young Harris would witness world-altering events in the 1730s and 1740s that would shape the colony of Pennsylvania, the frontier where he lived, the trade between the Whites and the Native Americans, and the outcome of the French and Indian War. Harris Jr. was just ten years old when Pennsylvania brokered the Walking Purchase Treaty with the Delaware Nation in 1737. The treaty established what the chiefs would give to the "White Fathers" and what they would keep in exchange for a clear boundary between the two groups. The treaty was faulty from the beginning. There was deceit and deception on the part of William Penn's son that would sour Native American relationships with the Pennsylvania government for a very long time. The Walking Purchase would also pit the Delaware, the Iroquois, and the Onondaga nations against each other for years. These were all tribes that Harris Sr. traded with, and the Harris Sr. trading post was often the chosen place for conversations about the relationships between tribes and between Native Americans and White settlers.

Harris Sr. owned land at the confluence of the Juniata and Susquehanna Rivers in what is modern-day Duncannon. It was known then as Clark's Ferry. More importantly, it was a Shawanese village whose inhabitants numbered in the hundreds. The chiefs of that village went to Philadelphia in 1733 to ask the Assembly to halt Harris Sr.'s efforts to establish a home and trading post there, due to the sacred nature of the land. The Assembly granted Chief Sassoonan and Chief Shikellamy's request based on previous deeds signed by the Penns and twenty-three chiefs of the Onondaga, Seneca, Oneida, and Tuscarora nations in 1732.[4]

Harris Sr. was never able to finish the work he had begun on the acreage he owned in that region, a concession that enabled the Assembly to keep the peace on the frontier. Harris Jr. was just eleven years old and was already learning about life on the frontier and the significance of treaties, deeds, and negotiations among the Whites and the Native American nations.

It was into this world of trust and turmoil, balance and bickering, friend and foe, provincial government and native government that the young John Harris Jr. would be forced. In 1748, he was given a commission as an ensign in the Provincial Army of England in Pennsylvania. He was elevated to captain less than one year later, when the previous company captain was moved to a different post. Harris Jr. turned twenty-one in October of that year, and in December, his father suddenly died, thrusting Harris Jr. into the position of sole inheritor of the entire Harris estate. In those days, the oldest child inherited all of the possessions of the father. His mother, Esther, had little say in the matter; it was a rule of law that left many women out in the cold or in untenable positions. Esther would soon remarry and leave the plantation. It is suspected that she did so because she and John Jr. could not see eye to eye.

Harris Jr. was now the owner of over eight hundred acres that existed on both sides of the Susquehanna. This acreage included his father's cabin, the tavern, several outbuildings, wagons, riding

---

4 George H. Morgan, *Centennial: The Settlement, Formation, and Progress of Dauphin County, Pennsylvania, from 1785–1876*, (Harrisburg, Pennsylvania: Telegraph Steam Book and Job Printing House, 1877).

horses and pack horses, for or five Black servants, his mother and his younger brothers, animals, as well as a licenses to trade, operate a tavern, and run a ferry across the river. While the 1740s were somewhat peaceful for Harris Jr. and the settlement of Harris' Ferry, there was a storm on the horizon that would wreck the plans of many a White, Black, and Native American person.

It was during this time of adjustment to his new position in life that John Harris Jr. married. Remembering that the total population of Harris' Ferry was relatively small—there were approximately 465 taxable landowners registered in 1750[5]—it would not be odd that a young woman would catch the eye of a young man who had newly come into wealth and position.

A man like Captain John Harris Jr. was surely the talk of the sewing circles. Mothers and fathers alike would have had a keen interest in seeing their daughter be the one to marry such a promising man. As for the young ladies, we can only suppose that Harris Jr., being a rugged and strong man, a captain by rank, and a community leader by status and possession, would be a prime catch.

It was Elizabeth McClure, the daughter of Richard and Esther McClure of Paxton,[6] who would capture the eyes, heart, and soul of young John. Her father was a prominent individual in the settlement of Harris' Ferry and a contemporary of John Sr. Richard McClure's name appears in the 1750 list of taxable landowners mentioned above. Elizabeth was born on the frontier in 1729, and therefore would have been familiar with the workings of a plantation like Harris's. She would have been properly taught how to run and manage a home inside and out, including gardening, washing, cooking all kinds of wild game, making clothes, weaving baskets, cutting hair, caring for animals, butchering and rendering, preserving, candle making, and more.

John and Elizabeth most likely had known each other for years and may have gone through the traditional country courting process. The use of bed boards, bundling bags, and courting candles were all possible. I feel certain that Richard and Esther McClure

---

5 George H. Morgan, *Centennial*, 16–20.
6 "Elizabeth Harris (McClure)," www.Geni.com, a genealogy website.

agreed with the match. After all, John was wealthy and had rank, status, position, and prospects. There were very few men on the frontier who could match the status and wealth of John Harris Jr.

Elizabeth McClure and John Harris Jr. went to the Rev. John Elder of the Paxton Presbyterian Church to be married. The year was 1749. John was just twenty-two, and Elizabeth was twenty. The thought that everyone married young because people grew up fast and did not live long (life expectancy in the eighteenth century was around forty-five years of age) was just not true. Many young men wanted to establish themselves before marrying, and that took time. Usually, a man was in his early twenties before he ventured out on his own. For young women, the courting process that began at fifteen or sixteen could quite possibly last four or five years. By the time an engagement took place and a reading of the banns was scheduled and occurred on a Sunday morning in church, several years could have passed. John and Elizabeth had done their due diligence, and the time had come for a proper wedding.

Historical romantics contend that Harris Jr.'s first marriage was one of love and deep connection. Harris Jr. had found not only his mate in life but someone equal to the task of frontier living. She was strong and resilient. She was born into the frontier life and knew it well, which was just what John Harris Jr. needed in a life partner. He would spend days on the road, riding back and forth to Philadelphia, and he would spend many nights away from Elizabeth, negotiating trade with Native American nations or brokering new land deals. Whoever married entrepreneur and businessman John Harris Jr. would need to be able to handle life alone, as he was carving out a name for himself that would eventually become the foundation for the name of the capital of Pennsylvania.

Chapter 3

THE EARLY YEARS

In the years leading up to the French and Indian War in America— or what was known globally as the Seven Years' War—John Harris Jr. had done the hard work of positioning himself as a pivotal player in the conflict. He had been promoted to the rank of captain of the ranger militia, one of several captains on the western frontier. He had expanded the ferry business, developed his land, bought even more land, and he was uniquely aware of the condition and positions of most of the tribes in Pennsylvania. He was well acquainted with travel throughout Pennsylvania, and the Pennsylvania government in Philadelphia saw him on a regular basis.

In the early months of 1753, Harris Jr. had journeyed west in an effort to secure trade and to reconnoiter the condition and situations of the Native American tribes and assess the status of their allegiance to the Crown. News that the French were pushing into the Ohio Territories had begun to reach Harris' Ferry via traders of the Ohio Company, who had gotten into scuffles with French soldiers. In a letter of concern written to the Pennsylvania governor, Benjamin Franklin writes:

On May 22, 1753, Governor Hamilton informed the Assembly that a large army of French and Indians had passed Oswego on its way to the Ohio Country. England's Indian allies there would be forced to withdraw and English traders would be captured and their goods destroyed. This report, which came from Governor Clinton of New York, was confirmed by Andrew Montour, who had been at Onondaga, where the Six Nations were alarmed by the French invasion.[7]

A week later, "the House heard testimony from James Galbraith, a justice of Lancaster County, John Harris, of Harris' Ferry on the Susquehanna, and Michael Teaff and Robert Callender, Indian traders, all of whom had just returned from Ohio."[8]

The Pennsylvania Assembly decided to assist the traders and England's Native American allies in hopes that strengthening those arms into the western frontier would make the colony stronger as a whole. Supplies such as muskets, gunpowder, flints, tomahawks, baking flour, and rum were shipped to Harris Jr.'s house to be distributed as needed to maintain the fragile alliance.

Harris Jr., who was busy building a business and taking charge of this new and fledgling outpost on the Susquehanna, was traveling west for weeks on end. This left Elizabeth to raise Mary and Johnny and manage the Harris plantation by herself. Her mother-in-law was remarried and was living in Silver Spring township on the western shore.

People on the frontier came to each other's aid. Most likely, Elizabeth would have received help from her mother, who may have moved in with her while John was gone on these adventures, especially when they involved John's work with the colony of Pennsylvania.

Returning home, Harris Jr. went back to his business ventures. He had, after all, a ferry across the Susquehanna to run, a trading

7 "Pennsylvania Assembly: Reply to the Governor, 31 May 1753," *Founders Online,* National Archives, https://founders.archives.gov/documents/Franklin/01-04-02-0180. [Original source: *The Papers of Benjamin Franklin,* vol. 4, *July 1, 1750, through June 30, 1753,* ed. Leonard W. Labaree. New Haven: Yale University Press, 1961, 500–502.
8 Ibid.

post to maintain, farmland to care for, a fur trade to manage, and a tavern to operate. Records show that Harris Jr. got into a bit of trouble that year. In August 1753, he was found guilty of keeping:

A tippling house without being first recommended by the Justices of Lancaster County at their Quarter Sessions or Court of record for the same County to the Licenter and Governor of the Province of Pennsylvania of his licence [sic] for so doing or without obtaining such licence [sic] and then and there without such recommendation or Licence [sic] did sell and deliver and cause to be sold and delivered to sundry Persons diverse Quantities of Rum, Beer, Cyder & Whiskey by less Measurer than one Quart each and Wine by less Measure than one gallon.[9]

It would seem that Harris Jr. was selling liquor by the glass and in effect, running a bar out of his tavern without a license from the colony. The document does not stipulate the fine or the process of correcting the fault. It would seem that Harris Jr. most likely obtained the needed license and went on with business.

I would like to add an interesting side note that came up in the papers I have studied. Harris Jr. is often listed as "John Harris of Paxton Township in Lancaster County, yeoman." This designation as "yeoman" places him squarely in the social class between laborers and gentry. Yeomen were usually landowners and most likely did farming as well. Harris Jr. held a position of respect and influence.

At the end of 1753, the Assembly gave Harris Jr. an official assignment. He was to travel west from Harris' Ferry to Logstown (the present-day Ambridge) on the Ohio River, just north of the confluence of the three rivers in what is Pittsburgh today.

The task given him was a part of a much larger project of the Pennsylvania government to control the wilderness. Harris was to note the distances between known markers along the route between Harris' Ferry and Logstown and report his findings to

---

9 Lancaster County Historical Archives.

the authorities in Philadelphia. There, the information would be compiled with other routes being collected on the Pennsylvania frontier by other traders in an effort to map the wilderness and expand settlement. I mentioned this event previously, but it bears repeating due to its significance.

Harris set out in 1754 and kept a journal of the route as he made stops at familiar places along the way. It is hard to imagine that Harris would have made the trip alone. It is supposed that he would have taken with him one of his trustworthy manservants. "Negro servants" Jack or Issaac would have been accustomed to traveling with Harris on the road from Harris' Ferry to Philadelphia. The Kings Road from Philadelphia split in two, with one route going through the city of Lancaster and the other, through the city of Reading. Harris was known to use both routes, depending on the business dealings he had at the time. Seldom was the trip challenging, and usually it included an overnight stay in a tavern or with friends in either of the two towns mentioned. Traveling alone was not recommended, for multiple reasons. Men and women traveling solo were known to be attacked, robbed, and even killed.

Horse travel could be challenging at times—there is no shortage of historical reports of persons who were injured or killed in horse accidents. Harris may have taken one of his sons, Johnny or David, with him as a way to introduce them to trade and business as well as to the rigors of eighteenth-century travel. How else does one learn the family business but to accompany Dad? The hours spent in a saddle provided time for long, in-depth conversations. That is how Harris Jr. learned from his father, and now his sons would learn from him.

So, when Harris was asked to go to Logstown and to note the mileage from one stop to the next, he was more than capable. He could travel relatively unafraid. As a licensed Indian trader, he was known by most of the tribes and was seen as a good and trustworthy White man. His dealings with tribal leaders gave him the opportunity to rub elbows with chiefs, such as Half-King of Logstown, and high-ranking tribal delegates who would come to Harris's trading post to exchange furs for other goods.

Because of his status, Harris and his party would receive a warm welcome among his Native American friends. He would check on the tribal leaders to see how life was going in their worlds. He might inquire about how the game population looked and when the next hunting party was due to go out. He would ask what goods he should procure in Philadelphia and make available at his trading post in Paxton. And most significantly, he would learn that the French had been trading more heavily with the Native American population in western Pennsylvania, and that they were looking to establish a string of forts that would stretch from Canada to the joining of the three great rivers in what is now Pittsburgh.

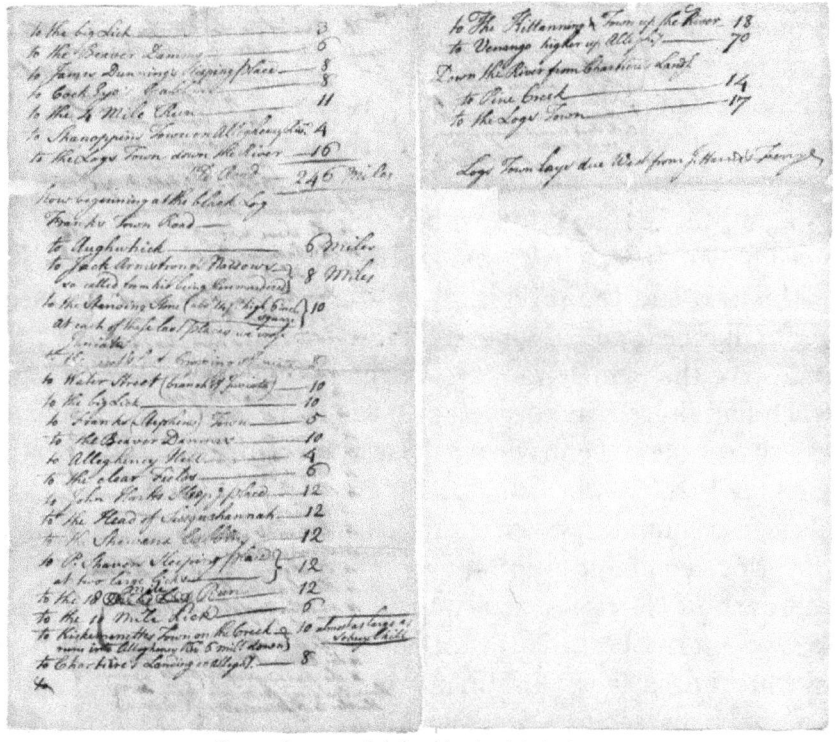

Pages in one of John Harris Jr.'s ledgers.

Harris took a southerly route from Paxton to Logstown that took weeks and covered 246 miles. This route would be the same one British General Forbes would take in his successful effort to take Fort Duquesne from the French in 1758. This same path would become the route of the South Penn Railroad and the Pennsylvania Turnpike. Harris also reported a second way to journey to Logstown via a more northerly route that was calculated to be 220 miles. Horse travel was the standard method of tracking milage in those days.

A horse that could reliably travel fifteen miles a day was the tool for calculating the distance from point A to point B. These horses were so well known by their riders that they could estimate the distance they had ridden in an hour, based on terrain, weather, and the pace and stride of the horse. In a world where horses were used daily as a form of travel, most people could gauge a trip on how long it would take a given horse to make the journey. To us this might sound more than just a bit inaccurate. Who judges distance by how far a horse can go in an hour? But based on the recorded distances given by Harris on the Logstown trip, we discover an incredible accuracy. No distance is more than a half a mile off one way or the other, and the total trip was within one mile of the actual distance as we know it today. How's that for historical accuracy?

This trip and the several others that would be undertaken by traders like George Croghan, Andrew Montour, and John Pattin would give the Pennsylvania government ample evidence that the French had indeed encroached into what was considered to be the western frontier of Pennsylvania. Harris had already reported to the Assembly in 1753 where the boundary was located, based on the milage from both Raystown (near present-day Altoona) and Frankstown (located about five miles southeast of present-day Altoona). Records show Harris was at a council in Logstown from May 12–25, 1753.[10] Some modern-day historians presume that Harris may have run into the party of Virginians, including George Washington, who were being led by Croghan, Chief Half-King, and Christopher Gist. While Harris knew the latter three individuals personally, he was not familiar with the young Virginia officer who was leading the trek. As of yet, there is no documentation in any writings from

---

10 Pennsylvania Provincial Council Records, vol. 5, p. 614–615.

the time period proving that Harris and Washington were introduced, but there are comments describing Harris's interaction with Montour, Gist, Croghan, and Half-King during this trip.

According to Pennsylvania Provincial Council documents, Harris returned from Raystown with his report in just two days on this trip.[11] That is a 126-mile trip on horseback. I have ridden on horseback, and I find it hard to imagine riding over sixty miles a day. Yes, it is possible to do so, but it is truly challenging physically, and it must have been hard, even on the twenty-six-year-old Harris. This is the kind of accomplishment that makes someone like Harris a hero to those of us today who can barely imagine themselves managing the normal daily tasks of eighteenth-century life.

So that we do not lose the humanity of heroes such as Harris, let me add some facts we know about daily life in Paxton. After Harris Jr. settled the John Harris Sr. estate with his mother, who was now Esther McChesney and was living in Newberry Township in Cumberland County, he was responsible for the care of his underage brothers. His receipt books record payments for board and schooling for both David and Samuel in 1753 and 1754. Most likely, these would have been private arrangements with the teachers, one named Thomas Alleosand[12] and the other, Isaac Baker. Schools were scarce on the frontier. Sending a young boy off to a boarding/schooling situation assured a good education and therefore, a good future.

It was also in 1753 that Harris paid one pound and ten shillings to renew the patent for the ferry he operated across the Susquehanna. In that same receipt book is the recorded purchase of multiple bundles of furs as well as the fee paid to one Mr. William West, a teamster, for carrying them to Philadelphia. Harris also logged the purchase of twenty bushels of malt, obviously for the making of beer.

On top of all of his government and business dealings, Harris maintained his plantation. In 1753, he and Elizabeth had a three-year-old daughter, Mary, a two-year-old son, Johnny, and they were expecting son David, who would be born in February 1754. I have no illusions that life on the frontier was anything but

---

11 Pennsylvania Provincial Council Records, vol. 5, p. 762.
12 Spelling is uncertain.

difficult, and yet, the relatively normal aspects of life, love, and living—repairing a broken section of fence, making bread, feeding animals, plowing and harvesting, enjoying a book with a cup of tea—were present in ways that make the Harrises' "usual" everyday life much like ours.

Within months, however, normal life on the Susquehanna would vanish when war knocked on the door of the Harris household and the community of Paxton and Harris' Ferry. Harris Jr. would play a central role in the French and Indian War in Pennsylvania. His house and trading post would become a place of negotiations as well as a stronghold, housing troops and supplying the frontier.

Chapter 4

THE FRENCH AND INDIAN WAR

The year 1754 brought dynamic change to the frontier of Pennsylvania. Harris had returned from the Logstown trip and soon traveled east to Philadelphia to report his findings to the Assembly. Afterward, he returned home to await news of what to do next.

Harris's records still exist today and are in storage for safekeeping—because of the fragile nature of the laid linen paper—at the Pennsylvania State Museum in Harrisburg. They reveal the seasonal work of tending a farm.

During planting season, there was plenty of work to be done by everyone on the plantation. Fields needed turning, seed needed planting, and fences needed to be checked and repaired. People who needed to cross the river and trade, now that the weather had started to turn, were showing up at Harris' Ferry. The local tribes were beginning to move about as well. War parties and trading parties alike made their way to trading posts like the one Harris owned along the Susquehanna River. Harris was a trusted individual, born and raised on the river. The tribal leaders knew him as one who would be fair and generous. Trappers and hunters with furs stacked high on the backs of pack horses also showed up at Harris's trading post, looking for goods (the preferred payment for furs) or coins.

Trading was the best way to get what was needed on the frontier. Selling furs for coins meant that a trapper then had to turn those coins into goods or food stuffs. It was much easier to trade furs for cloth or for a Dutch oven—or better yet, for a musket or a tomahawk. Harris's own account books show entries in 1754 for items like a carriage and the prime, or average cost of a hogshead of rum (£21 on April 13) and a barrel of rum (£5 17s. 9d. on April 22).

Native American and White traders alike who came to Harris's trading post brought news from every corner of the frontier west of Paxton—including stories of the incursion of the French into the three-rivers area near Logstown. There were stories of trade talks between the French "fathers" (the king and other political officials) and the chiefs of some of the tribes as a way for the French to gain allies in the Ohio county. Many of the tribes had allegiances with the British through previous treaties made in places like Albany and Lancaster. They felt they could not side with the French because they would be breaking the treaty with their British fathers. Once a treaty had been reached, the word of a chief and the intentions of a tribe were binding, even when the other side was not holding to its part. This level of integrity was seen as admirable by some Whites, and it was abused by others, who tested the limits of the treaties by not adhering to them and upsetting the Native American nations. It also led to a loss of trust that the Whites would keep their promises, which, at times, created an undercurrent of distrust among the tribal leaders. Some of them had ears for the French promises, which were coming in waves.

Word of the conversations the French were having with tribal leaders at Logstown got back to John Harris through the trappers and traders, both Native American and White. Concerns began to grow in the spring of 1754. Their fears were justified. News traveled that a young lieutenant colonel from Virginia, who had barely survived an adventure into the wilderness of western Pennsylvania the year before, was venturing back into the frontier again. He had hired George Croghan and Half-King to guide him and to parlay with tribal leaders with whom Lieutenant Colonel Washington was unfamiliar. Half-King was ready for war. His hope was that this young officer from Virginia would allow him to paint his tomahawk red with the blood of the French.

On May 24, Edward Shippen of Lancaster wrote to Benjamin Franklin Esq.:

> *Dear Sir,*
> *The inclosed came to hand just now, which I send to you, to let you see the Spirit of some of our back Setlers [sic]. If the Managers of the Lottery for the Battery should think Proper to encourage those People, they may be pleased to send fifty small Arms to Captain John Harris, who ought to engage himself to see them forthcoming. I am out of all Temper with our Assembly; but have a great esteem for yourself and am Dear Sir, Your Most Humble Servant.*
> *Edwr. Shippen*
> *Ps. I am just setting off for Cumberland County and shall call on Captain Harris and let him know what I have done with his Letters.*[13]

Harris's plantation was to become a supply depot for the frontier. This arrangement with the Pennsylvania Assembly would continue into the American Revolution.

On May 28, just four days after the letter from Shippen to Franklin, the party of Virginians and Native Americans came upon a group of French, and it was Lieutenant Colonel Washington who began the skirmish. But it was Half-King who ended it by placing his tomahawk into a not-yet-dead French officer named Joseph Coulon de Villiers de Jumonville. This brutal act touched off what would become known in the American colonies as the French and Indian War, which was about to impact the daily life of Harris, his

---

13 "To Benjamin Franklin from Edward Shippen, 24 May 1754," https://founders.archives.gov/documents/Franklin.

family, and the people of Harris' Ferry.

As news traveled to Harris' Ferry that Lieutenant Colonel Washington was digging in at a place called Fort Necessity, people on the frontier became increasingly nervous. Most had interacted with Native Americans, and many had built deep friendships. Now there were rumors that some of the Pennsylvania tribes might side with the French. If the alliances collapsed and friends became enemies, life in the wilderness of the western frontier would go from peaceful to chaotic in no time at all.

On July 3, 1754, the French took Fort Necessity, sending the provincial soldiers running for their lives. Washington returned to Williamsburg, Virginia, where he immediately resigned his commission in the army.

This political cartoon was published in Benjamin Franklin's Pennsylvania Gazette.

On July 10 of that year in Albany, New York, a plan to unite the colonies was adopted. The "Join or Die" cartoon came out of the Albany Plan of Union and was printed by Benjamin Franklin in the

Pennsylvania Gazette. A new wind was beginning to blow in the colonies, and men like Harris would have to deal with the massive change it would bring. No one would be untouched by the changes that were about to come.

A group of Harris' Ferry settlers formed to discuss their concerns. A fair portion of the economy of the Paxton settlement depended on a secure and peaceful western frontier. The threat of war meant a disruption of trade and the flow of goods that people depended on for their livelihoods. Harris owned thirteen outbuildings on the plantation, which were used to store the furs and agricultural goods that came to him from the west. His ferry business would also suffer if people stopped traveling back and forth from the frontier.

Harris was one of a group of fifty-six men who gathered to draft a letter to Deputy Governor James Hamilton in Philadelphia. Their request was obvious: allow us to defend ourselves by supplying us with munitions. The letter read:

> The humble petition of the inhabitants of the townships of Paxton, Derry, and Hanover, and Lancaster count, humbly sheweth [sic], that your petitioners being settled on the near the river Susquehanna, apprehend themselves in great danger from the French and Indians, as it is in their power several times in the year to transport themselves, with ammunition, artillery and every necessary, down the said river—and their conduct of late to the neighboring provinces, increases our dread of a speedy visit from them, as we are as near and convenient as the provinces already attacked, and are less capable of defending ourselves, as we are unprovided with arms and ammunition, and unable to purchase them. A great number are warm and active in these parts for the defence [sic] of themselves and country were there enabled so to do, (although not such a number as would be able to withstand the enemy). We, your petitioners, therefore humbly pray, that your Honor would take our distressed

condition into consideration and make such provision for us as may prevent ourselves and our families from being destroyed and ruined by such a cruel enemy; and your petitioners, as in duty bound, will ever pray.[14]

The letter was signed by all fifty-six men and sent to Philadelphia, where it was read in Pennsylvania Provincial Council on August 6, 1754. It was up to the council to decide how the frontier would be managed and preserved. While people on the frontier waited nervously for its ruling, they returned to normal life. Harris's logbook notes that he bought a sorel mare for £6 on September 3 and paid his subscription to the Rev. John Elder, costing £3. Subscriptions like this covered the church's operating costs, including maintenance of a pastor. Parishioners who paid enough could be given a particular seat or box in the church. Harris was a staunch supporter of the Paxton Presbyterian Church.

As October rolled around, life at the Harris plantation took an interesting turn. On the first day of the month, a band of Native Americans showed up at Harris's plantation from various tribes in need of help. Harris knew all of them as friends and partners in trade. They had fled from the misfortunes of Washington as he battled French troops. Their claim was that Washington was a nice enough man but did not treat the tribesmen well nor consult with them as he should have.

Half-King (also known as Tanaghrisson or Tanachrisson or Tanacharison) had fallen ill with what is believed by many to have been pneumonia and needed care. He was accompanied by family members as well as several other prominent chiefs of the Six Nations, which included Monacatootha (or Scarouady as some knew him). Monacatootha was with Washington at the defeat of Jumonville, the spark that lit the fire. Half-King did not survive his illness and died at Harris's home. Monacatootha assumed Half-King's role as the lead speaker for the Six Nations. Again, Harris was at the center of pivotal moments in history. Information

---

14 George H. Morgan, Centennial, 21–22.

collected from family histories in Ancestry.com tells us:

> On the 1st of October 1754, Tanachrisson, or Half-King, a noted Indian chief, died at Harris' after a few days illness. He was buried about where the Mulberry Street school house is located, in the English manner, *"much,"* says John Harris, in a letter to the Provincial authorities, *"to the satisfaction of his friends."* Monacatootha, a chief of the Six nations, accompanied him. Two years after this celebrated Indian also died at Harris'. No mention is made of this fact in the Provincial Records, but in the receipt book we notice, John Graypeel [Graybill] promises *"to Deliver in good Order to Adam Torance in Lancas'r, at Frederick Yelser's [Welser], three Guns, three cut lasses, 3 old Matchcoats, one Bundle of Sundrey's wrapped in an Old Blanket, Belonging to Monacatootha, Deceas'd."*[15]

Another receipt refers to the burial of the Half-King. Harris wrote to the Assembly and Governor Morris on October 29, 1754, that Half-King had died at his place and that he buried him properly, while Monacatootha *"set off for Aughwhick."* Harris was left caring for the Half-King's family, which he said he would do "till they be removed." He sent a bill to the Assembly, and on December 17, 1754, the Committee of Accounts reported that they would pay Harris the amount he was due, "plus £5 for his troubles." That Half-King was taken to Harris's home and his family and tribe trusted Harris to care for him and bury him is not inconsequential. It once again shows us Harris's place as the hub of a great wheel that had spokes reaching out in every direction.

The conflict with the French ebbed as combatants slipped into "winter quarters"; armies in the eighteenth century held off on major interactions with enemy troops in the harshness of winter. Harris went back to work on the plantation. On the same day that he wrote the letter asking for compensation for caring

---

15 George H. Morgan, *Centennial*, 189.

for Half-King and his party, Harris also traded a horse for "100 weight of fall deerskins at Abrm. Mitchell."[16] A month later, on December 9, he paid for a carriage coming from Philadelphia with "2 hogsheads rum." [17] At heart, Harris was a businessman and an entrepreneur, and the winter months were a great time to do paperwork and make trade deals with other businessmen in places like Reading or Lancaster or on the docks and taverns in Philadelphia. Those months allowed for repairs to tools and equipment and butchering—since meat could hang without spoiling like it would in warmer weather. Winter was also a time to sit by the fire, mending clothes or repairing leather horse and carriage tack.

However, spring brought a new level of conflict, and the people of the greater Paxton area began to feel the pain of war, many on a very personal level. Stories started reaching Harris' Ferry of attacks by small bands of Native Americans called war parties, which traveled light and fast. Their tactic was to hit quickly and move on, disappearing into the woods. Even so, Harris Jr. stayed busy doing business. His account book lists a purchase of a hogshead of West Indies rum for his tavern on June 5, 1755, for £15.[18]

The councils in Pennsylvania, Virginia, and New York, as well as the British Parliament, agreed that it was time to remove the French army from the western frontier. General Edward Braddock was sent west with regular troops, state militia, provincial troops, and native allies with the goal of engaging the French.

Braddock was ambushed on July 9, 1755, and received the wound that would end his life. This victory gave the French and their Native American allies all the encouragement they needed to branch out further and wreak havoc on the settlers and farmers who had moved into the fertile frontier land in western Pennsylvania. Those war parties began to reach further east, into the small communities in the counties of York, Cumberland, Berks, Northampton, and Lancaster (the upper Dauphin

---

16 Pennsylvania Archives, John Harris Receipt Books 1749–69, vol. 1.
17 Ibid.
18 Ibid.

area). Harris Jr. knew people and had friends living in those places. Conrad Weiser was at Harris Jr.'s house on July 9, discussing the recent events of war, when they received word of Braddock's defeat.[19] The news was a serious blow to those who lived on the Susquehanna and west. Their confidence in their safety was shaken. Weiser returned in August and again on September 7, accompanied by a leading chief called The Belt, due to the increase in hostilities.[20]

The mangled bodies of those who had been killed were sent to Philadelphia to arouse the Assembly to do something. On July 24, 1755, Governor Robert Hunter Morris called the Assembly to action. It was time, in his words, due to "the cruel incursion of the French and barbarous Indians, who delight in shedding human blood."[21] By October, the world was in flames. Incursions by the native war parties were reaching further east, and news from the frontier was getting worse. Settlers were leaving their homesteads and moving east to the safety of larger, more populated towns. Word had gotten out to Lieutenant Colonel Washington that several significant chiefs were at John Harris's homestead, and he was hoping to draw them into service against the French and their Native American allies.

On October 16, a war party of Native Americans who had partnered with the French brought devastation to the small community of settlers living along Penn's Creek, just north of Paxton. A band of Delaware swept into the small village. Of the thirty-four inhabitants, fourteen were killed, scalped and mutilated, and twelve others were taken into captivity. Captain Harris, along with forty-six other men from Harris' Ferry, headed north to bury the dead. They met with Shikellamy and Old Belt, two chiefs, and to then went on to Shamokin to learn as much as they could about the raiding party.

George Washington wrote that on October 17, 1755, he

---

19 George H. Morgan, *Centennial*, 23.
20 Pennsylvania Provincial Council, *Minutes of the Provincial Council of Pennsylvania*, vol. 6, 551 and 613, https://play.google.com/books/reader?id=j00OAAAAIAAJ&pg=GBS.PR16.
21 Pennsylvania Provincial Council, *Minutes of the Provincial Council of Pennsylvania*, vol. 6, 485, https://play.google.com/books/reader?id=j00OAAAAIAAJ&pg=GBS.PR16.

received correspondence from *"Mr Harris at Susquehanna."* [22] The letter contained valuable information concerning where the various tribes were located and their movements. He advised the colonel that Old Belt or Belt of Wampum was at his plantation along with other important Native American leaders. On October 18, Washington dispatched Christopher Gist to Harris's homestead in hopes that he would be able to convince those tribal leaders to join Colonel Washington in his efforts to squelch the concerns on the frontier. Gist was also tasked with finding Andrew Montour and a company of Native Americans who would join the efforts. [23]

Conrad Weiser saw this as an explosive time and wrote to James Read, Esq., in Reading that he should *"make preparations to stand the enemy, with the assistance of the Most High."* [24] By then the news of the Penn's Creek massacre had traveled far and wide. And again, Conrad Weiser was on his way to Harris' Ferry to discuss the next steps.

Meanwhile, men from Harris' Ferry plantation were traveling home from Sunbury on October 25. They were advised to travel on the east side of the river. But Harris and the others were skeptical and decided it was a trap. So, they went down the west side of the Susquehanna and right into an ambush. The account is written by Adam Terrance, one of the men on the trek, and it was attested to by ten others, including John Harris's brother William and the Rev. John Elder. The account includes the almost instant deaths of four men on the opening volley of gunfire and of another, who was chased down into the river and *"struck with a tomahawk on the head."* [25] Benjamin Franklin was informed immediately because of his government position as the person in charge of Native American affairs and forts on the frontier. When the account was written, there were nine in the party who had yet to return home. John Harris Jr. was one of them.

---

22 "Letter from Geo. Washington to Robt. Dinwiddie," Founders Online, https://founders.archives.gov/documents/Washington/02-02-02-0115.
23 Ibid.
24 George H. Morgan, Centennial, 27.
25 *The Pennsylvania Gazette*, October 30, 1755, 2.

It took four days for Harris Jr. to return home, as he was avoiding Native American scouts who were tracking him. Meanwhile, Franklin's *Pennsylvania Gazette* reported, *"It is supposed John Harris is dead."*[26] Of course he was not dead, much to the joy of Elizabeth Harris and their children. But this was close enough for John. He needed to take action, and so he did. He wrote to Edward Shippen on October 29, *"I have this day cut loop-holes in my house, and am determined to hold out to the last extremity."*[27] On October 31, Harris wrote to Benjamin Franklin from his plantation home, saying that information from Andrew Montour convinced him that the settlement at Paxton was in imminent danger of an attack.[28] He informed Franklin of his concerns and the increasing danger. He explains that if it had not been for the journey up to Shamokin, which revealed the incursion of Native Americans, they would not have discovered it *"till put in Execution."* The Native Americans allied with the French planned to push into the Susquehanna Valley, and their plan was proving successful.

Included in Harris Jr's letter to Shippen were a call for Conrad Weiser to come to Harris Jr's homestead immediately and the news that espionage on the frontier was alive and happening. Harris Jr. stated: "I have sent out two Indian spies to Shamokin; they are Mohawks." According to an October 31 letter from Harris to "all His Majesty's subjects in the Province of Pennsylvania, or elsewhere," the two Mohawks traveled to Harris Jr's home with Andrew Montour and Belt of Wampum along with "other Indians."[29] In an effort to keep him aware, on November 1 Christopher Gist wrote to George Washington from Philadelphia, saying that he was on his way "to meet with the Natives, Montour, and Weiser at Harris' Ferry."[30]]

It is important to note just how significant Harris' Ferry and John

---

26 Ibid.
27 Franklin Papers, *Founders Online.*
28 Franklin Papers, *Founders Online.*
29 George H. Morgan, *Centennial*, 27.
30 "To George Washington from Christopher Gist, 1 November 1755," *Founders Online,* National Archives, https://founders.archives.gov/documents/Washington/02-02-02-0159. [Original source: *The Papers of George Washington*, Colonial Series, vol. 2, *14 August 1755–15 April 1756*, ed. W. W. Abbot. Charlottesville: University Press of Virginia, 1983, 154.]

Harris Jr. himself were to the future hopes of peace on the frontier of Pennsylvania. To underscore the level of significance they held, here is a letter written on December 1, 1755, by Gov. Robert Hunter Morris to the Provincial Council, a group of delegates designated to oversee the expenditure of military funds.

> Gentlemen,
>
> *Upon considering the state of our friendly Indians on the river Susquehanna, I think it necessary that Messengers should be immediately sent to convene them to come down to Harris's Ferry in order to concert measures with this Government upon the present Circumstances of affairs when it may be proper to communicate to them such parts of the General Plan of operations as they may assist in the execution of.*
>
> *I am Gentlemen Your Most Humble Servant*
> Robert Hunter Morris[31]

By the end of December, a detachment of thirty men with Captain James McLaughlin in charge was sent to Harris' Ferry by Governor Morris to support the settlers.[32] Things were beginning to heat up, but the end of the war was several years—and a lot more bloodshed—away. People Harris knew personally lost their lives, and Harris's life was in grave danger. No one traveled anywhere without firearms at the ready. The peace that had been so diligently labored for by Harris's father, John Harris Sr., and the other settlers on the Susquehanna had gone from fragile to completely broken.

Hostilities slowed down in the winter of 1755–56. It was common for whole armies to go into winter quarters due to the

---

31 "Robert Hunter Morris to the Provincial Commissioners, 1 December 1755," *Founders Online*, National Archives, https://founders.archives.gov/documents/Franklin/01-06-02-0122. [Original source: *The Papers of Benjamin Franklin*, vol. 6, *April 1, 1755, through September 30, 1756*, ed. Leonard W. Labaree. New Haven and London: Yale University Press, 1963, pp. 284–285.]
32 "To Benjamin Franklin from Robert Hunter Morris: Commission, 5 January 1756," *Founders Online*, National Archives, https://founders.archives.gov/documents/Franklin/01-06-02-0139. [Original source: *The Papers of Benjamin Franklin*, vol. 6, *April 1, 1755, through September 30, 1756*, ed. Leonard W. Labaree. New Haven and London: Yale University Press, 1963, pp. 342–348.]

challenges presented by foul weather. Flintlock muskets were less dependable than usual in poor weather. The cold required bundling up, which made it harder to move or fight. Livestock was much harder to keep, move, and maintain during the winter months. And feeding an army was challenging when the weather was good. During the winter months, armies resorted to foraging.

Harris was at home, taking care of his large plantation. He owned land on both sides of the Susquehanna as far north as modern-day Duncannon and as far south as modern-day Goldsburo, Pennsylvania. With the birth of William on January 23, 1756, Harris Jr. was now the father of four. Between Harris Jr.'s own receipt books and the Colonial Records of Pennsylvania, we discover that Harris' Ferry was abuzz with activity, again underscoring the importance of John Harris's settlement on the Susquehanna.

Conrad Weiser made it to Harris's homestead for a meeting called for by the governor. It was January, and Whites and Native Americans alike traveled in the harshness of the bleak midwinter to discuss what they would do come spring. Several tribal chiefs were in attendance, and their names were listed in the Colonial Records of Pennsylvania—names such as Satacaroyies, The Belt (of Wampum), Garisdsoney, Aroas, Broken Thigh, and Newcastle. This posed a threat to the tribes that were aligned with the French, and a war party was sent to kill the chiefs at the meeting. The war party was intercepted and repelled on January 31.[33]

In March 1756, things were getting "dangerous" at John Harris's homestead.[34] Tensions were rising throughout the colony of Pennsylvania, as the coming of spring set new war parties in motion. Harris built a stockade around his home, tavern, and storehouses and posted a permanent guard. On April 10, 1756, Harris joined George Croghan and Teedyuscung (otherwise known as the king of the Delawares) for a trip to Fort Allen in Northampton/Lebanon County. Their task was to escort Col. William Clapham and his company of soldiers west to the Susquehanna. By May, the situation

---

33 Colonial Records of Pennsylvania, vol. 7, 33–34, https://archive.org/details/colonialrecordsov7harr/page/n54/mode/1up.
34 Ibid, 57.

was so perilous that Governor Morris went to Carlisle and then to Harris' Ferry to assess the needs of the people and to establish his plan for the defense of the frontier.

Clapham, Morris, Croghan, and Harris met at Harris's homestead to work out the design for Fort Hunter, Fort Halifax, and Fort Augusta, which were to be built as soon as possible as part of the defense of the whole colony. Colonel Clapham probably was the officer sitting at the table who marked Elizabeth Harris as a strong and capable woman. As a result of that meeting, by June Harris' Ferry had been turned into a storehouse for munitions, including muskets, cannons, powder, flints, and more. More than a hundred soldiers were camped along the Susquehanna. War was knocking on Paxton's door, and settlers were leaving the frontier in droves.

By the end of 1756, more than a hundred people had left the frontier and moved back east. Many of these people had come to the wilderness of Pennsylvania because of John Harris and the stability that he provided at Harris' Ferry. Now they were leaving, and Harris felt a tremendous burden. So, instead of backing off, he kicked it into a higher gear and began to do more. In a time when his life was threatened and his future was unsure, Harris stepped up and gave his all. His storehouses expanded with military supplies bound for "Armstrong's Battalion: 20 blankets, 2 barrels powder, 2 casks lead."[35] On October 14, 1756, Adam Reed, a prominent member of the Harris' Ferry community, sent a letter to Edward Shippen and "Fellow Subjects" of Pennsylvania. He wrote of death and destruction and of those who had been carried off by the Native Americans as captives. In the postscript to the letter, Reed wrote, "Before sending this away, I would mention, I have just received information that there are seven killed and five children scalped alive but have not the account of their names."[36]

Captain Harris marked his thirtieth birthday in 1757. He was married to the love of his life and now had four children. He now held almost one thousand acres and a plantation that included a home, a tavern, multiple outbuildings and storehouses, pack horses and

---

35 John Harris Receipt Books, 1749–1769, Pennsylvania State Archives.
36 George H. Morgan, *Centennial*, 33–34.

wagons, and a ferry business across the mile-wide Susquehanna River. There were times when he must have felt the weight of the world on his shoulders…yet he pushed on and continued to answer the call.

Thank God he did, because 1757 was going to be the worst of times on the Pennsylvania frontier. While there was a cessation of hostilities during the winter months, the spring season brought the horrors of war once again. A Great Council was called for, and everyone was to gather at Harris's. The Colonial Records of Pennsylvania lists 160 Mohawks, Oneidas, Tuscaroras, Onondagas, Nanticokes, Cayugas, Delawares, Senecas, and Conestogas, with their women and children. The English delegation included George Croghan, William Pentrup as interpreter, James Armstrong, Hugh Crawford, Thomas McKee, and Deputy Governor William Denny. The Council began gathering in March, and by the end of May, an agreement had been reached with the Delaware and Shawanese tribes to end aggressions against the settlers across the frontier.[37]

Accounts in the *Pennsylvania Gazette* state that only days before the agreement was reached, eleven persons were killed at Paxton. After the treaty, Harris wrote to Deputy Governor Denny, "The Indians here, I hope your honor will be pleased to be removed to some other place, as I don't like their company."[38]

Harris stayed active as the businessman he was at heart. His receipt book states that he was shipping goods to Fort Augusta as well as buying things like hides, sugar loafs, fish, flour, and salt. His operation would transport these items from the docks in Philadelphia by wagon or pack horse to Harris' Ferry, where he would store them and ship them out as requested to Forts Halifax, Hunter, Augusta, and Ligonier.[39]

The tension settled for only a few months and then rose again in August, when almost twenty persons were killed in Paxton. Women and children were taken captive, houses and barns were burned, and cattle were killed.[40] The scene was horrific and left fear in its

---

37 Pennsylvania Colonial Records, vol. 7, 489, 506–507, 597. And George H. Morgan, *Centennial,* 33–34 and 190.
38 George H. Morgan, *Centennial,* 195.
39John Harris Receipt Book, 1749–1769, Pennsylvania State Archives.
40 George H. Morgan, *Centennial,* 34–35.

wake, which is exactly what the Native American attackers were hoping would happen.

By October, the frontier looked like a ghost town, and John Harris was not only concerned but truly saddened that the conflict had had this kind of effect on his friends and neighbors. People fled for their lives and left everything behind. This once-thriving settlement was now empty, and the remaining people were living in fear as they moved into survival mode. Many, like Harris, had shifted their business interests toward the war effort. Supplying an army is not an easy task. Shoes, clothing, tack and shoes for horses, musket repair, transportation of goods and supplies, and of course, food. All of this was a massive undertaking.

Earlier in the year (on March 29, 1757) the Assembly had passed an act "Forming and Regulating the Militia of the Province of Pennsylvania." Up to six thousand men were employed in the task of protecting and defending the colony and preserving the rights and privileges of its inhabitants.[41] These provincial troops were divided into three battalions and numerous companies. Harris remained a captain in the militia. His home became a fort and outpost. Colonel Clapham wrote: "I shall leave a sergeant's party at Harris, consisting of twelve men, twenty-four at Hunter's Fort, twenty-four at M'Kee's store, each under the command of an ensign: and Captain Miles, with thirty men, at Fort Halifax, with the inclosed [sic] instructions, as I have removed all the stores from Harris Ferry and M'Kee's to this place."[42]

During 1758, there was a general exhaustion with the situation on the western frontier and in the Ohio Valley. The British government sent the entire command of General Forbes, which included over 6,200 men. Provincial and regular soldiers, militia, highlanders, and allied Native Americans all converged on the western frontier by first crossing the Susquehanna River at Harris' Ferry. Forbes was given the tasks of taking Fort Duquesne from the French and running the French back up to Canada. Harris was given the task

---

41 William Clark, *Official History of the Militia and the National Guard of the State of Pennsylvania*, (Philadelphia: C.J. Hendler, 1909), 12–16.
42 George H. Morgan, *Centennial*, 51.

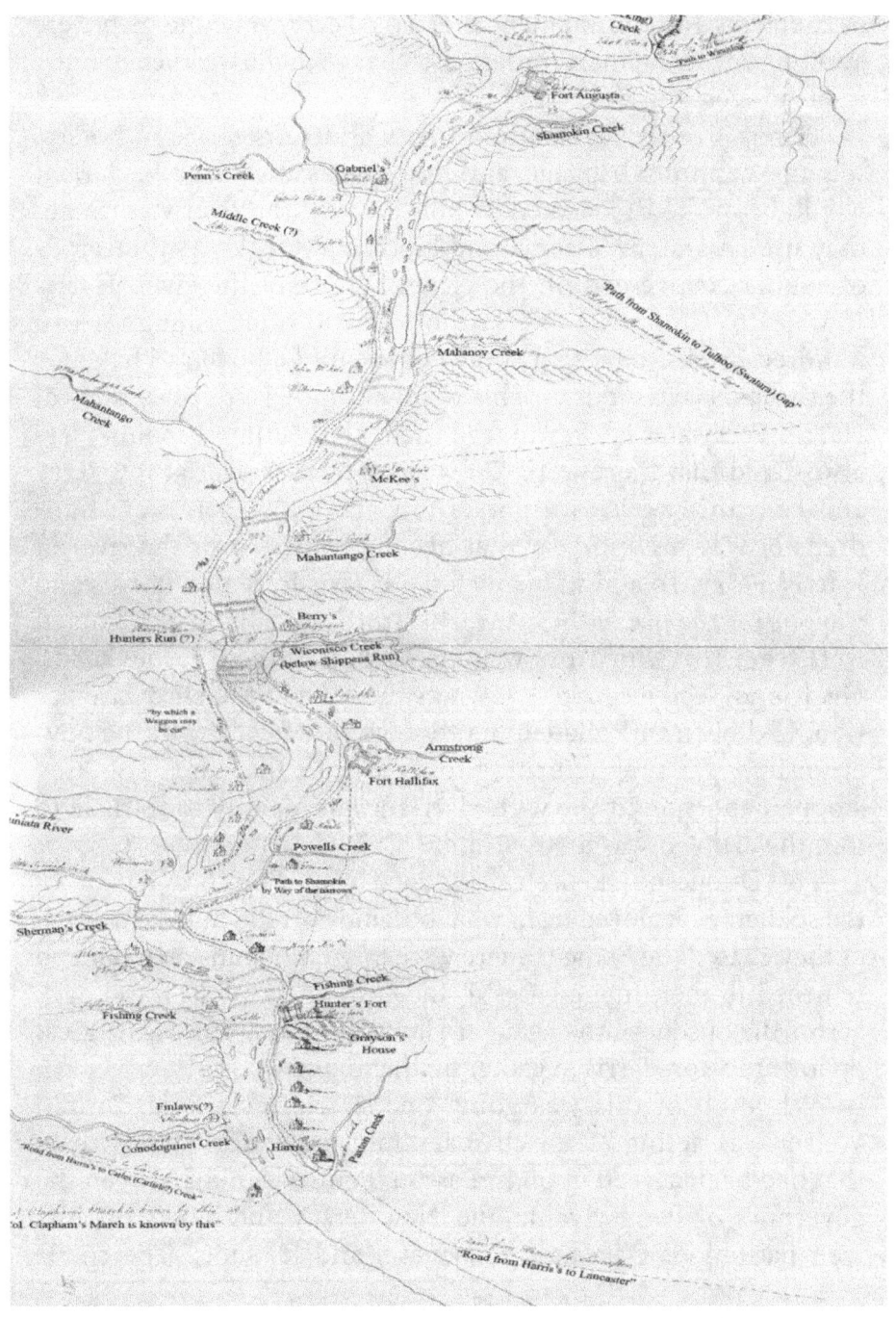

Joseph Shippen's map, drawn in 1756.

of supplying the encampment at Harris' Ferry while the men were awaiting either their next orders or a change in the weather, making it safe to cross the river.

Harris Jr. used flat-bottom boats and rafts to carry horses, wagons, cannons, baggage, and more across the river. Each boat would be pushed/navigated by pole arms. If the river was rough, they used a system of ropes and block and tackle. As thousands of soldiers converged on the eastern shore of the river, Harris Jr. wrote to Colonel James Burd on May 8, 1758, asking for two hundred bricks to be sent so he could build an oven to bake for the troops. Harris Jr. found himself with thousands of soldiers at Harris' Ferry and no way to feed them all in a timely manner. He also stated that there were "70 wagons to pass over at my Ferry and Falls this week with horses to Carlisle."[43] There were hundreds of wagons and gear that needed to pass over the river at Harris' Ferry. To add to his income, Harris Jr. rented horses and wagons for the use of the army. His brothers William and Samuel were teamsters who drove wagons west on the new Forbes roads. His friend Teedyuscung, known as the king of the Delaware nation, had been in Philadelphia to negotiate peace with the governor and was now returning to fight with the army. The king stopped and spent time with Harris Jr. on his way to Carlisle to join the army. It was a busy time.

Fort Duquesne had been abandoned by the French, and many of the soldiers redeployed from what became Fort Pitt and went north as they chased the French. There were many who mustered out and returned to their home bases to the east. They would travel back across the Susquehanna again at Harris Jr.'s ferry. This was a great opportunity for Harris to gather firsthand news.

While all of this was going on, Harris Jr.'s friend Conrad Weiser was acting as the primary interpreter for a new treaty that had been agreed upon in Easton, Pennsylvania, between the governors of Pennsylvania and New Jersey and chiefs of thirteen nations of Delaware, Shawnese, and Iroquois. The chiefs

---

43 John Harris Receipt Book, 1749-1769, vol. 1, Pennsylvania State Archives.

agreed not to fight with the French against the British in exchange for the return of large tracts of land in Pennsylvania that had been ceded by the Iroquois, plus the vows to honor tribal hunting grounds and not to establish colonial settlements west of the Allegheny Mountains. With the fall of Fort Duquesne and the signing of the Treaty of Easton, people began to breathe a bit easier. Upward of 80 percent of the White settlers of the frontier had fled east, and now, at the end of 1758, they could start moving back to their homes and farms.

John, Elizabeth, and their four children would spend the next several years in relative quiet, considering the past years of intense activity and fear at the Harris plantation. While the war moved north through New York and up into Canada, life returned to normal for the Harrises. In 1759, John found himself in a positive financial position, and it was time to expand the business and get ready for an influx of people moving west again.

Chapter 5

YEARS OF PAIN AND PROGRESS

For several years, there would be relative peace on the frontier of Pennsylvania, except for the occasional bear or buffalo wandering into the city or the excitement of the shad run on the river each year. There was also the cry of another child to John and Elizabeth. Named Elizabeth, she was born on November 22, 1759, but she did not survive for long. There is no death date given for Elizabeth; we know only that she did not live long enough to count the days. In the eighteenth century, even when the best of care was available, the loss of a child was common.

For those who were living out their lives in places where the only healthcare was the collective knowledge of those who lived nearby, infant mortality was high. The lack of prenatal care, difficulties or complications during the birth, diseases with no known cures, and little to no medical knowledge all contributed to the deaths of many babies born on the frontier. While the Harrises were by no means alone in their grief, the impact must have been life-altering for parents and siblings alike. In the following year (1760) death would strike again,

Harris Jr. lost his brother William, who was living in Elizabethtown with his wife and son.

The relative peace that came in 1760 did not last long. The Native Americans began an attempt at pushing back the settlers who were moving west, disrupting the peace that had been arranged at Easton a few years earlier. Chief Pontiac led a movement that would once again see people on the frontier being killed or captured. Raiding parties moved freely in Cumberland and Lancaster counties and encroached into towns like Reading and Lancaster. The activity was in full swing in 1762. By 1763, most people were frustrated beyond what they could endure. In '62 "Brother Onas," a term used by the Leni-Lenape in reference to the Penn family, recommended John Harris Jr.'s trading post as the official trade store for Native Americans.[44] Pontiac's Rebellion, as it became known, affected the people of Harris' Ferry deeply.

Friends and relatives were losing their lives, their homes, and their children. The Quaker-led government tended to seek peaceful resolutions, but Native Americans continued to harass the settlers, and tensions grew daily. In September, the Provincial Assembly took action. Harris Jr. wrote to his friend Colonel Burd in November that, "His honor, the Governor, has allow'd £25 for each scalp. £30 for each Indian prisoner."[45]

Looking back, it seems inevitable that some who were fed up with life on the frontier would light the powder keg. Harris believed the situation could easily get out of hand, and he was right. A band of renegade men from the Paxton Militia, of which Harris Jr. was an officer, was bent on eliminating a group of Native Americans who were being held at Conestoga. In December 1763, this band, known as the "Paxton Boys," went to Conestoga and savagely murdered the tribesmen who were being housed there, even after multiple attempts to cool these hot heads. Their complaint was that these Conestoga Native Americans were secretly

44 Brother Onas, August 27, 1762, Colonial Records of Pennsylvania, vol. 8, (Harrisburg: the State of Pennsylvania, 1838), https://archive.org/details/colonialrecordsov5harr/page/753/mode/1up, 754.
45 "Letter from John Harris to Col Burd at Fort Augusta, Nov. 20, 1763," Colonial Records of Pennsylvania, (Harrisburg: the State of Pennsylvania, 1838), https://archive.org/details/colonialrecordsov5harr/page/753/mode/1up.

supplying other Indians and deviously raiding around the county, which was not true.

Harris Jr. was not a part of this band of out-of-control vigilantes. He and the Reverend Elder spoke out against the action but were implicated by association. Because Harris Jr. believed that the delicate relationship between the Whites and Native Americans needed to be strengthened and maintained, he called on the Colony of Pennsylvania to do all in its power to resolve the problems and reinstate the peace. Eventually, Harris Jr.'s name was removed from any and all accusations regarding the massacre at Conestoga. But Harris Jr. would soon have to deal with a more painful situation.

On January 20, 1764, he lost his wife, Elizabeth. Records tell us that she died at home but do not reveal the cause of death. She was just thirty-four years old, and she left behind four children. Mary was now thirteen; Johnny, twelve; David, ten; and William was seven. It had been just over four years since baby Elizabeth passed on. This leads us to believe that Mother Elizabeth's death was not connected to childbirth, as was common—unless she was pregnant again and died giving birth to an unrecorded child, with the child dying as well. This is speculation only. We have yet to uncover an official medical document giving us a cause of death, so all we can do is speculate. For all we know, an accident or a disease may have taken her life.

John was now left alone to raise his four children, manage six servants, run a tavern, operate the ferry business, and run the plantation. He had just lost the love of his life, to whom he had been married for fifteen years. The prevailing thought among some historians is that he carried her in his heart for the rest of his life and never recovered from her loss.

The death of Elizabeth not only left John with an empty place in his heart, but it also left the plantation void of her skill and direction. John depended on Elizabeth to manage the everyday activities of the house and gardens, the greater farm tasks, the care of the children, and the stores and supplies. She was essential to the sunrise-to-sunset operation of the Harris complex. A plantation like Harris Jr.'s was a self-sustaining enterprise. The food planting, growing, harvesting, preparing, and preserving that kept the family and servants fed was a major undertaking, let alone the mending of garments, the cleaning, the washing of bed clothes, and overseeing the servants' workday duties.

The Colonial Records of Pennsylvania and Harris Jr.'s own receipt books show almost no activity for the first half of 1764. Harris Jr.'s operation was still the central hub for supplies going out to the frontier forts. The Harris plantation was also a meeting place for the officers of the provincial army, who came and went with regularity, based on the recorded correspondence that identifies Harris Jr.'s plantation as the point of origin of their letters.

Harris Jr.'s receipt book has an entry in June 1764, documenting that he paid £58 1s. for his daughter's schooling and clothing to "M.. Clark." This is one of the first glimpses of Harris Jr.'s belief that girls should be educated just like boys. Mary had turned fourteen in April. This may have been payment for her graduation, since most girls who were educated would have finished school around the age of fourteen.

If losing Elizabeth was not enough, on July 3, 1764, William died. He was the fourth of their five children, and he was just eight years old. There are no records telling us how or why he died. Nothing in John's account or receipt books mentions the loss. We can only imagine the heartbreak John was going through. He had lost baby Elizabeth; his wife, Elizabeth; and now William, who was just coming of age. Surely John would have taken William out fishing and hunting. Did they begin the discussion about his schooling and education while walking along the river? Mary, Johnny, and David were all still young and at home…how this death must have affected them, we can only guess.

Due to the intense need for a helpmate and partner in life, Harris Jr. would court and marry the daughter of Adam and Mary Reed of Hanover Township. Adam, a contemporary of Harris Jr.'s father, was prominent in Paxton and instrumental during the French and Indian War. Mary, his daughter, was born in 1730, making her thirty-four years old. In '64 John was thirty-seven and in need of a mother for his children, a manager for the plantation, and a life partner for himself. They married in November of '64. It is not known whether Mary Reed had been married previously. There is no listing of children whom she brought to the marriage, so we are led to believe that if she was married previously, she had no children. Being close in age and closely connected in the community, we can only presume that John and Mary knew each other prior to the death of John's wife Elizabeth. This may have been one of those fortuitous opportunities that seldom comes along in life. Or possibly, they felt as though they were guided by a divine hand.

Shortly after his marriage to Mary, Harris Jr. began planning to build a new house. This structure would sit back from the bank of the river on higher ground than the old homestead built by his father. The old house, as well as the tavern and storehouses and outbuildings, would continue to serve multiple purposes. A man of Harris Jr.'s stature needed a house to match his position and status. Both of his older sisters were married and doing well for themselves. His three younger brothers had also made names for themselves. He no longer needed to look after any of them. As a matter of fact, he was now Uncle John to several nieces and nephews.

He navigated all of this while serving on the Pennsylvania Proprietary and Governor's Council in Philadelphia. In 1764, there was an effort in government to end the proprietary government that had been established by the Penns and move to a royal government. This change would take a whole lot of power from the Penns. The efforts failed, and the Penn family, primarily Thomas Penn, stayed in position.

At home, Harris Jr. was committed to building what would be as grand a house as any that might be found in Philadelphia. This would be a statement that all would see. Clearly, Harris Jr. was telling the world that he had made his mark, and it was time his home represented his status. It would be a very large stone house with three floors and a cellar. There would be four rooms on the first floor, laid out in a square with a central hallway. The second floor would be a mirror of the first floor, consisting of four rooms. The third floor or attic would have five rooms. There was to be a separate outdoor kitchen close by but independent of the main house, as well as a barn, stables, and an outhouse.

While we are not exactly sure when the plans were drawn up for the house, we know that construction began as early as 1765 and was in full swing in 1766. The largest sums were paid to two masons (Able Rees and John Davis) and a carpenter (John Doharty) for their work on the stone house and kitchen. They received £220 and £340, respectively. Harris also hired Crush and Abram Wood to "measure the house and expenses."[46] They would, in effect, be the project managers. To give some kind of modern-day perspective, the average worker in the eighteenth century could expect to make £50 to £150 per year. A business owner who produced goods like shoes or barrels could expect to earn between £200 and £500 per year, depending on the town he lived in, supply and demand, etc. The masons and carpenter made a year's salary on one job—Harris Jr.'s house. That would not be so amazing if the house were in Philadelphia, but such a thing happening on the frontier once again put John Harris Jr. on the map. He was recognized as a forward-thinking investor and entrepreneur, a statesman and politician, a friend to Native Americans, and faithful to his God. All of this, and he was not yet forty years old.

Business took off in the later part of the 1760s, as the repeal in 1766 of the controversial Stamp Act (1765) settled tensions that were rocking the colonial nation. As the owner of a trade store on the Susquehanna, Harris Jr. was deeply affected by the decisions coming out of Parliament in London. Each pound spent at his store meant more he would be sending to England in taxes. As a good Englishman, his parents both being from Yorkshire, Harris Jr. believed that surely the British government had the colonies' best interests in mind while also trying to recoup the massive amount of money it had spent on the French and Indian War in North America. Harris Jr. saw himself as a good British subject, but there was a restlessness stirring in the colonies, fueled by a group called the Sons of Liberty.

The Pennsylvania Colonial Records tell us that Harris Jr. was instrumental in the establishment of a post rider, who would make regular deliveries between Harris' Ferry and Lancaster town. News would now travel a bit faster, and it was good that it did. In an effort

---

46 Wm. C. Armor, *The John Harris Mansion, 1766–1897*, (Harrisburg, Pennsylvania: Harrisburg Publishing Company, 1897), 2.

to force Great Britain to stop taxing the colonies, the dock workers in Philadelphia enacted a ban on importing goods from England for about six months in 1769. Every order Harris Jr. made for English goods was halted or turned away in the Philadelphia port where he did all his business. This halt in the flow of goods meant that everything the colonists were required by law to buy from England rather than manufacture in the colonies (such as window glass) was stuck on a ship and could not be offloaded in Philadelphia. Shop and tavern owners like Harris Jr. had to wait it out creatively. Fortunately for Harris Jr., the supplies he needed to finish the house had arrived long before the blockage of goods.

The John Harris-Simon Cameron Mansion. (Cameron, a US senator, owned the house in the late nineteenth century.)

John and Mary's new house was completed by the end of 1768, according to his account book, in which he recorded settling all his debts for the house. Total cost, £1132 3s. 10d. By modern-day standards, it was a mansion. The beautiful new gray-stone house faced south, with the front door looking across the mighty Susquehanna. The orientation was precise for a reason. The house pointed the way for thousands of travelers venturing into the furthest reaches of Pennsylvania. He named it "Compass House" as a way to show everyone that this house was the new center of the entire colony of Pennsylvania. He began to believe that the seat of government for the colony should be situated at Harris' Ferry.[47] He would eventually work tirelessly to make that happen.

By the time they moved into the new house, they had lost two children. Adam was born on November 7, 1765, almost one year to the day of their marriage. Adam did not live long. On February 15, 1767, James (the first child to whom they gave that name) was born and, like Adam, did not survive. So, while building the house, serving in government in Philadelphia, running the trading post, raising Mary, Johnny, and David (who were now all teenagers), managing the servants, and operating a ferry boat business, he and Mary also navigated the enormous grief of losing two children. When Mary and John were married, there was no record of Mary being previously married or bringing children with her. It was not until researching the 1780 Register of Negro, Mulatto, Slaves and Servants that we discovered Mary (Reed) was the widow of a slave owner.

Was she unable to have children with her first husband? Did Mary suffer from some sort of medical condition that would be easily cared for today? The limited medical knowledge and abilities in the eighteenth century, coupled with life on the frontier, makes it almost impossible to know. Whatever was going on, it must have been disconcerting to both John and Mary.

What we do know is that they kept trying to have children, and on September 5, 1768, Robert Harris was born. He would survive birth and grow into adulthood. John was forty-one and Mary was thirty-eight years old. They now had to keep up

---

47 Luther Reily Kelker, *History of Dauphin County, Pennsylvania*, vol. 2, (New York and Chicago: The Lewis Publishing Company, 1907) 501.

with a baby. The other children and servants would be helpful; still, there is nothing like a newborn to totally disrupt a home. On Sunday April 16, 1769, less than a year after Robert's birth, Mary, Harris Jr.'s oldest child (with his first wife, Elizabeth), was married to William McClay. This marriage would begin a history-making relationship between McClay and John Harris Jr. with regard to the future of the city of Harrisburg and the establishment of Dauphin County.

While building his new marriage, his new house, his family, and the business, there were heart-wrenching challenges in Harris Jr.'s life. John lost a sister in 1768. Esther was married to Dr. William Plunket, who practiced medicine in Carlisle, Pennsylvania. They had four children. John then lost his oldest sister, Elizabeth, in 1769. Elizabeth was married to John Findley (Finley) and they lived in Harris' Ferry. She was forty-nine years old when she passed. She and her husband had six children.

To suggest that life in the eighteenth century—and especially on the frontier—was hard and filled with heartache may be an understatement. Harris Jr. was not immune to these trials. The lack of proper medicine, knowledge of diseases, proper hygiene, and safety precautions when working reduced the average lifespan, as did plagues like smallpox and childbirth complications.

In spite of all of the challenges, by 1770 John Harris Jr. had built a small empire on the Susquehanna River at the place where his father had thought best to put down roots. His name was now synonymous with one of the major jumping-off points into the West, making Harris Jr. one of the few men in Lancaster and Cumberland counties to have immense influence over the direction of the entire colony of Pennsylvania. He was a friend of every person of means and position—White and Native American—and was in good standing with officials in England. But all of this was about to change.

The peace that most all of us hope for in life was once again disrupted by sharp division. This time, Harris Jr. found himself on the wrong side of the divide—or in the middle—at least for a while. In the meantime, Mary was pregnant again. Their daughter, Mary, (his second daughter with that name) was born in October. She would grow into womanhood and be married to John Andre Hanna, a man of importance. But the coming events would force Harris Jr., his family, and the nation to decide whether to remain loyal to the Crown, and they would eventually lead to war.

On March 5, 1770, a series of events began that would inevitably lead to a revolution. The Sons of Liberty in Boston had been stirring up the population against the British Crown since the Stamp Act and the Townshend Act. Their anger was directed at anyone who represented the power of Parliament and King George III. That anger came to a head as civilians threw snowballs filled with ice at British soldiers, who were standing guard. The soldiers reacted by firing into the crowd, killing five people and kicking off a wave of bloodshed throughout the colonies.

Chapter 6

THE AMERICAN REVOLUTION

Harris Jr. had purchased the rights to the entire estate from his remaining siblings, who had come of age and were due parcels of land according to their father's will. In 1770 Harris Jr. was drafting a plan to create lots to sell in an effort to expand Harris' Ferry. He put the idea on hold as events continued to take place that made him uneasy. He would not give up on the idea of a bustling town on the Susquehanna as is evidenced by his "Lot Book," created in 1775 to track the lots and their sales. By this point in his life, he was bound and determined to follow through on the idea of a "grand town" on the Susquehanna that just might rival Philadelphia as the seat of government in the future.

During the years between 1770 and the official start of the American Revolution on April 19, 1775, Harris Jr. was very active. Business was booming, the farm and orchards were growing, and the Harris' Ferry trading post and tavern were becoming the hub of business in the colony of Pennsylvania. Trouble struck again, though, when his daughter Mary and her husband, William McClay, lost their first child in February 1770. They had named the baby after the founder—John

Harris McClay. But he did not survive. The McClays' daughter, Elizabeth—named after Mary's mother—was born on February 16, 1772. They nicknamed her Eliza. Harris Jr. was now a grandfather. Mary and William would go on to have seven more children, six of whom would live into adulthood. Harris Jr. and his wife Mary would lose two more infants as the colonies began to argue with the mother country. Jean was born on March 18, 1772, and Joseph was born on October 23, 1774. Neither survived.

As anger toward Great Britain grew in the colonies, Harris Jr. was in regular correspondence with Colonel Burd, Governor Morris, and the colonial government in Philadelphia. He had maintained a storehouse of munitions that functioned as an arms depot during the French and Indian War and Pontiac's Rebellion. These arms would be a valuable asset to the Pennsylvania government, and therefore needed to be kept safe and secure. Storehouses like the one at Harris Jr.'s plantation were strategically positioned in the colonies under the direction of the British government. It was common knowledge that the Sons of Liberty had been discussing the need for arms and a plan to raid the storehouses to gain them. After the "tea parties" in Boston and other cities down the East Coast in 1773, it was understood that this group of rebels would destroy property if it suited their cause. This raised a concern for everyone who was hoping for a peaceful resolution to the difficulties and grievances.

But in Hanover Township, a day's ride northeast of Harris' Ferry, a group of nine men had entirely different plans. In June 1774, this group met to draft what would become known as the Hanover Resolves. These resolves called upon the colonies in America to band together to oppose what they deemed to be "iniquitous and oppressive" actions. And if Great Britain continued to "force unjust laws upon us by the strength of arms, our cause we leave to Heaven and our rifles."[48]

Harris Jr. chose not to be a part of this call for separation. All of these men were important in Hanover Township and the greater

---

48 George H. Morgan, *Centennial*, 55.

Paxton area, and many were Harris Jr.'s friends. For a while, this move separated those who insisted on liberty from John Harris Jr., who was not only true to Great Britain, but a good English citizen. Harris Jr. held that Great Britain, with its well-trained army and massive naval fleet, was too large a power to engage. A few days later, his good friend Colonel Burd formed a group in Middletown and created a similar set of resolves. The call for liberty was too strong to be squelched by Harris Jr., and by December 1774, a general committee had been formed in Lancaster County made up of delegates from every township. If war was coming, the people of Lancaster County would be ready. Harris Jr. was not a part of the original formation in '74, but he was elected to serve on the general committee in '75. War was coming, and once again, Harris Jr. found himself right in the middle of it.

The shot heard around the world on April 19, 1775, was clearly heard by the Harris family. His two oldest sons, Johnny (twenty-three) and David (twenty-one) were eager to join the cause. Harris Jr. reprised his rank as captain and served as one in charge of organizing and equipping the men. The Associators, as they were known, since the colony did not allow militia units, would head out to Lancaster under other friends of Harris Jr.—Captain John Cook and Captain Matthew Smith. According to John Harris Jr.'s receipt book, they would meet up with Thompson's Battalion and Capt. John Paterson's Company of Associators.

On July 4, 1775, the people of Paxton, led by Harris Jr., raised £130 for the relief of the people in Boston. On that same day, David, with a commission, left with John to serve with Thompson's Battalion. Harris Jr. is quoted as saying, "I shall let my other son Johnny go cheerfully in the service anywhere in America."[49] This is where the story gets a little crazy. Historians claim that Johnny went with the rest of the Pennsylvania troops to Quebec, under the command of Generals Richard Montgomery and Benedict Arnold. It is thought that Johnny was killed at the battle of Quebec, but that is impossible. Not only was Johnny mentioned in John

49 William Henry Egle, ed., *Notes and Queries, Historical and Genealogical, Chiefly Related to Interior Pennsylvania*, (Harrisburg, Pennsylvania: Pennsylvania State Library, 1932), 333.

Harris Jr.'s will, but he was issued a pension for his time in service and for being wounded at the Battle of Paoli in September 1777.

Harris Jr. mentions in his receipt book that he had "offered David for service and Johnny for the Indian Warr." [50] It is very possible that Johnny never went to Quebec but instead stayed in the Paxton area or went to one of the other forts and served with the local militia against the Native Americans who had sided with the British. On July 19, 1775, Harris Jr. wrote to the Pennsylvania Assembly, "Keep the savage Nations engaged on our side will be of greatest service to our cause."[51] Harris Jr. was acutely aware of the importance of the Native American nations and made sure they remained allied with the Patriot cause.

It is also possible that young Johnny did go to Quebec and was captured—not killed—and paroled on August 6, 1776, with all of the others who had been captured,[52] and then made his way back to Pennsylvania and joined up with the Twelfth Regiment of Foot,[53] which would be joined with the Eleventh Pennsylvania Regiment that fought under General Anthony Wayne at Paoli. Historians who believe that Johnny was killed at Quebec argue that the "Captain John Harris" who was listed in the Eleventh Pennsylvania Regiment was Harris Jr. But at this point in his life, Harris Jr. was almost fifty years old. His task, at that age and stage of his life, was to supply the army as a recruiter, to store guns and ammunition, and to provide essential food stuffs to Washington's army at places like Valley Forge.

So, in unraveling the historical catalog as well as the official records, the conclusion is that there were two Captain John Harrises serving during the American Revolution. One was our very own John Harris Jr., who served as a supply captain from his home on the Susquehanna. The other was his son, Captain John Harris III, who served on the front lines of the war. I will say more about this as we look at Harris Jr.'s last will and testament.

---

50 John Harris Receipt Book, vol 2. 1760–1791 Pennsylvania State Archives.
51 Ibid.
52 "Dauphin County Pennsylvania in the Revolutionary War," New Horizons Genealogy, http://www. newhorizonsgenealogicalservices.com/pennsylvania-genealogy/dauphin-county/dauphin_county_pennsylvania_in_the_revolutionary_war.htm.
53 George H. Morgan, Centennial, 207.

Let us get back to the start of the conflict to look at the activities of John Harris Jr. as the pot began to boil over. Late in 1775, John was elected to serve in the Pennsylvania Congress, meeting in Philadelphia. He had been elected to serve as a representative from Cumberland County, since he was a landholder in that county. While there is no information or documentation that leads to this conclusion, we are left to think that it must have been easier for him to get elected in Cumberland County than it was in Lancaster County, which is where the plantation was located. Like many other people in the colonies, Harris Jr. was not in favor of going toe-to-toe with the greatest military force in the world. He was not convinced that a war to separate from Great Britain was a sound idea. After all, he was a good Englishman and had never had a grievance against the Crown. His taxes were not onerous, and there were no British soldiers quartered in Harris' Ferry.

The discussions in the beginning of 1776 must have been heated and passionate. Members of the Pennsylvania delegation to the Continental Congress were arguing for a Declaration of Independence. The Hanover Resolves had gone too far. Now, a declaration of utter separation from Great Britain? This was going beyond reason, in Harris Jr.'s mind. The rout of the British troops outside of Boston the previous year would not be tolerated by the Crown. King George would retaliate, and it would not be pretty. Harris Jr. voted against "independency," but he was outnumbered.

Harris Jr. found himself in Carpenter's Hall in June 1776 as a part of the Provincial Conference of Committees of the Province of Pennsylvania.[54] He listened to the debates concerning independence while a committee of five was drafting the Declaration of Independence just down the street. Once again, he was in close contact with Benjamin Franklin, who was determined to see a United States of America, a free and independent nation. Harris Jr. was back home when the *Pennsylvania Gazette* arrived at his plantation home on the Susquehanna. An account of the day says this: "When

---

54 "Birth of the Commonwealth of Pennsylvania," Proceedings of the Provincial Conference of Committees of the Province of Pennsylvania, (Philadelphia: W & T Bradford, 1776), 5, https://www.ushistory.org/pennsylvania/birth3.html.

independence was formally declared, he [Harris Jr.] read the Declaration from a Philadelphia newspaper to his wife in the presence of their son. When he had concluded it, he remarked, 'The act is now done, and we must now take sides either for or against the country. The war in which we are about to engage cannot be carried on without money. Now we have £3 thousand in the house, and if you are agreed, I will take the money to Philadelphia and put it into the public treasury to carry on the war. If we succeed in obtaining our independence we may lose the money, as the government may not be able to pay it back—but we will get our land.'"[55] His wife, Mary, agreed with the plan. He saddled up and took the money to Philadelphia and received certificates in return. He would get pence on the pound in return when the war ended.

His £3 thousand was no small amount. In an age when most individuals were making less than £100 a year, and a good tradesman or craftsman could pocket as much as £200–£300 a year at best, Harris Jr. and Mary had £3 thousand lying around the house that he could sacrificially spare for "the Cause." Let us all clearly understand this fact before we go any further. Harris Jr. was extremely wealthy in comparison with the majority of people alive in the colony of Pennsylvania in his day. Let it also not get past us that he consulted with his wife to make sure she was in agreement on this plan to support the war. Not only was this an uncommonly egalitarian act for their day, but they also both knew what we sometimes miss in retelling history: the reason he consulted his wife was that any decision made by the husband had the potential to benefit or devastate the entire family. Mary needed to be aligned with Harris Jr. He needed her approval, knowing that she could end up withstanding the worst of the decision and would have the burden of making do if the Cause proved futile.

Harris Jr. most likely saddled up very early the next morning and headed for Philadelphia. We can presume that he took with him one of his male servants. They would make the trip in one day—not an impossible feat, but obviously a difficult one. It was

---

55 George H. Morgan, *Centennial*, 56–57.

no less easy for Mary, who was left behind with the children and the remaining servants to manage the plantation. Oh, and she was again with child and due to deliver in September. Harris Jr.'s oldest daughter was married and had three daughters of her own. His two oldest sons were fighting for the Cause and one of them was missing. Robert and Mary were just eight and six years old, respectively, and a newborn was on the way. Harris Jr. and his wife had their hands full as well as their hearts. To support the ragtag army was a risk, with so much on the line. But John was all in. He delivered the £3 thousand to Gov. Robert Morris himself the next day. He had been elected as an official electoral judge for Lancaster County and was a part of the drafting team for the Pennsylvania Declaration of Independence, just one of many local declarations that were written.

Harris Jr. was now fully engaged in the American Revolution as a person of political, economic, and social standing. Winning the support of John Harris Jr. was no small feather in the caps of people like Benjamin Franklin, who knew the weight and breadth of the frontiersmen who would come to the aid of their nation to win freedom and liberty. To have John Harris Jr. sign on meant they had a trusted and capable individual who could recruit, supply, and support the army from a vantage point deep enough in the interior that he might never engage British soldiers. Harris Jr.'s teamsters and his vast network of storage depots could keep goods and munitions moving to where they were needed. Harris Jr.'s connections with the Native American nations could potentially secure tribal alliances with the colonials. And having fought in the French and Indian War made him a seasoned veteran, who could be counted on in times of need.

Harris Jr. would manage his position as a supporter of the Cause as a member of the Pennsylvania General Assembly. He maintained close correspondence with officers whom he'd known personally for many years—men like Colonel William Cook, Major James Burd, Captain Armstrong, Colonel Hand, and of course, Edward Shippen, Esq. Many of the men from Paxton became part of the now-famous rifle battalions that were known for their ability to hit targets from as far as four hundred yards. Harris Jr.'s son David commanded a company and was the supply officer for the First Pennsylvania Regiment. To bolster support in Paxton, Harris Jr. read the Declaration of Independence from the front porch of Compass House, and he invited everyone to hear.

Johnny mustered back into the Twelfth Pennsylvania, which merged with the Eleventh and, later on, with the Ninth and served in the Philadelphia campaign. It was during this campaign that Johnny would be wounded at Paoli. Most of the wounded were cared for by British surgeons and then released to return home. Between the hardships of the Quebec campaign and the wound he received at Paoli, Johnny was a shell of the man he had been when he left Harris' Ferry for service in the war. John Harris Jr.'s last will and testament provides evidence of Johnny's lack of ability to care for himself. It reads:

> *I give and bequeath to my eldest son John Harris the sum of five pounds in species to be paid at my decease and all my wearing apparel and I do authorize and direct my Executors herein after mentioned to supply him, the said John Harris, with food and clothing and other necessier to the amount of thirty five pounds species per annum during his natural life to commenis from the time of my decease, and also in all cases of affliction whether of body or mind to recommend him to the care of my Executors, and more particularly to the care of David Harris and Mary McClay. The said legacies to be in full of all claims which he the said John Harris or any person or persons under him may or shall have against any part of my estate real or personal.[56]*

Harris Jr. ensured that his physically and emotionally broken son was well taken care of. Johnny would live until 1807 and die at the age of fifty-six.

But Johnny's condition was not the only hardship of 1777. On August 17, Harris Jr. and Mary lost little William, who was less than

---

56 John Harris Jr.'s last will and testament is preserved at the Historical Society of Dauphin County.

a year old. The cause of death, like all the others, is not noted anywhere that I have been able to find. Once again, the difficult life on the frontier exacted its price on the Harris family.

Harris Jr. stayed engaged in the political process. He remained an assemblyman, serving from Cumberland County, with a designation of being from the township of Paxton.[57] Because he was listed as being from Cumberland County, I was at first skeptical as to whether this was our John Harris Jr. or not. I knew he owned land in Cumberland County, which is why he was able to serve as a delegate from that county, but I was not sure that there was not another John Harris living in Cumberland County at that time. When the Assembly placed everyone in their township designations, Harris Jr.'s name moved from Cumberland County to Paxton Township. This gave me the clarity that I needed to be assured that the man listed as a delegate was, indeed, our John Harris Jr. During this first year, he was called upon to take part in drafting Pennsylvania's Constitution. This is said to be one of the most unique constitutions, with no governor and no senate. This photograph shows the Pennsylvania Constitution, which is kept in the Museum of the American Revolution in Philadelphia, open to the page that includes John Harris's name at the top of the list of delegates from Cumberland County.

John was appointed as a regional election judge for Lancaster County during the 1776 session. He made regular reports on the amount of shot and powder and the number of weapons in stores he was keeping at his plantation. He regularly found himself in Philadelphia, and in 1777, was appointed to the Committee of Fifty. This committee's task was to manage the supplies that were currently held in the Commonwealth of Pennsylvania and to move them to places where they could be stored safely and discreetly. Harris Jr. was a natural choice for service in this way. His knowledge of the roadways, storehouses, and merchants between Philadelphia and

---

57 "Birth of the Commonwealth of Pennsylvania," Proceedings of the Provincial Conference of Committees of the Province of Pennsylvania, (Philadelphia: W & T Bradford, 1776), https://www.ushistory.org/pennsylvania/birth3.html.

the Susquehanna River was unequalled. His years of trade in Reading, Lancaster, Philadelphia, and all points west of the Susquehanna made him invaluable during the war.

In 1778, his position was put to the test in huge ways. A British- and Loyalist-supported Native American uprising in the Wyoming Valley of Pennsylvania caused a mass exodus of settlers from the northern and western branches of the Susquehanna, heading south. They boarded boats of every size and condition and fled to Harris' Ferry as reports came flooding in that farmers, families, and soldiers were being slaughtered without quarter of any kind. It was known as "The Big Runaway." Harris' Ferry was jammed with those who had fled the massacre. Hundreds of wagons, along with boats, canoes, and rafts brought destitute people to Harris Jr.'s front door, looking for food and shelter. His son-in-law, William McClay, found himself smack in the middle of the mess. He wrote, "I never in my life saw such scenes of distress. The river and the roads leading down it were covered with men, women, and children flying for their lives."[58] And Harris Jr. engaged in helping this vast number of refugees of war who landed on the shores of the Susquehanna in Paxton.

In that same year, Harris Jr. recorded something that allows us some insight into life at Harris' Ferry. In his account book dated August 1, 1778, he logged giving something called "Freedom Clothing— If I had served him the Term of indenture." The clothes were for a man named Thomas Doherty. He had been indentured to Harris Jr. and was now released. Indentures were contracts of service for a fixed amount of time, often based on the sum of money the indentured person needed paid off. The freedom clothes were a gift that was commonly given by owners to their formerly indentured servants. Sometimes tools, dishes, cook wear, seeds, or even farm animals were also given as a way to kick-start the person's new life.

Many people who hoped to live prosperous lives in the colonies entered into contracts of indenture with someone who could pay their way from places like Ireland, Scotland, or Germany. Once they

---

58 Carl Lamson Carmer, *The Susquehanna*, (New York: Rinehart, 1955), 133.

landed in Philadelphia, they would work off the cost of the trip. The government set the number of years of service based on the price paid; between five and seven years were normal lengths of indenture. Harris Jr. was known to have indentured at least two Irish girls for his wife's use during the 1750s and 1760s. Until recently, we knew nothing of Thomas Doherty's existence. Most likely he was an Irish lad who wanted to come to America and make something of his life. He could not have chosen a better master than John Harris Jr. Thomas would have been well cared for with food, clothing, an education, and a comfortable place to sleep and call his own. Harris Jr. was known to be overly generous (go back and read his obituary) to those who were in his care.

It was also in 1778 that Harris Jr.'s wife, Mary, became pregnant again. Records show that the boy child was born on October 5, 1778, but did not survive. They gave him the name Read (or possibly Reed). Once again, the Harrises' lives were overshadowed with the grief that comes with the loss of a child. At this point, they had lost six children. John was fifty-one years old and Mary, forty-eight—beyond what most of us would consider child-bearing age. This is another glimpse into colonial life and life on the frontier in Pennsylvania. While my desire is to write an account of the life and times of John Harris Jr. based on solid research and historical documentation, I will go off my notes and into the world of conjecture for just a moment here. It is my opinion that there was very little to do once the chores of the day were completed. Like people who have loved each other throughout history, passions are not easily squelched, and candlelight and darkness give way to moments of intimacy.

I would have assumed that Mary had begun menopause, which may have made her think she would not become pregnant, but I am not a physician. Remarkably, she conceived again and lost a daughter in October 1780. They named her Elizabeth. Thankfully, in 1782 Mary, now 52 years old, delivered a boy who survived. They named him James. Harris Jr. went to great efforts in his last will and testament to make sure James was cared for and educated. Mary was fifty-two when James was born, and

Harris Jr. was fifty-five. From this point, there are no more children recorded.

During the entire American Revolutionary War, Harris Jr. was busy supporting the war effort from his home on the Susquehanna and from his Assembly seat in Philadelphia. He was re-elected to his seat in 1778, 1779, 1780, 1781, and again in 1782. We are told that while he was serving in the Assembly in April 1779, his horse was stolen. The Pennsylvania Colonial Records show that the horse was returned to him twenty-five days later.[59] I'm not at all sure why the records show that his horse was stolen and returned, except that it was newsworthy that it happened to an assemblyman. In these same records, he is referred to as "Major John Harris." Nowhere else is this rank alluded to in any documentation that I have uncovered so far. On looking into it a bit further, the reference is to a gun repair done by his brother, Samuel Harris who was a known gunmaker and repairman. This cross reference to his brother is evidence that it was our John Harris Jr. who was given the rank of major, quite possibly for his meritorious service during the Cause. Whatever the case may be, the rank does not seem to follow him. Nowhere else is it mentioned.

Harris Jr. served in the Pennsylvania Assembly from 1776 to1782—the entirety of the war. He received a handsome sum of money for his service and his travel back and forth to Carpenter's Hall in Philadelphia. Records show Harris Jr. receiving £970 for serving for seventy-three days and £675 for travel expenses. He was also "ordered to return 40 rifle musquets to be delivered to Mr. Samuel Hodgson" in Philadelphia.[60] Harris Jr. complied. And why not? The war had ended, and there was no longer a need to warehouse the guns at his place in Paxton. Finally, there was a sign of peace in the land. He could use the space that the munitions had occupied—there were lots of new ventures in his world. He took some time to be a husband, father, grandfather, farmer, tavernkeeper, ferryboat owner, trading-house manager, and politician. But it was also time to start building the new world, and he knew just where to begin.

---

59 Colonial Records of Pennsylvania, vol. 11, 87 and 760.
60 Ibid.

A photo of the registry page on which Mary and John Harris Jr.'s slaves are listed.

Harris Jr. was a central part of the new beginnings, and Pennsylvania would lead the way for the rest of the states. In March 1780, Pennsylvania was the first state to enact a Gradual Abolition Act. The war had highlighted the idea that those who were crying for freedom were in fact enslaving others. The abolitionist movement had a strong presence in Pennsylvania, and this group pressed for reforms that had been scratched from the Declaration of Independence to appease Southern colonies. The act stated: "Every Negro and Mulatto child born within the state after the passing of the Act (1780) would be free upon reaching age twenty-eight."[61] When released from slavery, they were to receive the same freedom dues and other privileges, such as tools of their trade, as servants bound by indenture for four years. Slaves were to be registered by November 1780, and those not recorded were to be set free. The bill passed with a vote of 34–21. No longer were children slaves for life simply because their mothers were slaves… that rule ceased to exist immediately.

And while it would take years for many enslaved people to realize their freedom, the system had been enacted that would lead the way for all persons in Pennsylvania to be free and the institution of slavery to be abolished for good.

---

61 Colonial Records of Pennsylvania, vol. 15, 9.

Chapter 7

NATION BUILDING

John Harris Jr. had committed to carrying out the dream of those who saw the Susquehanna as the spot for as handsome a town as could be situated in the state. He had these intentions before the Revolutionary War interrupted his thoughts. In his mind, he believed Harris' Ferry was the hub of a great wheel that made up the whole of the commonwealth. And he would do his part to make Harris' Ferry into Harrisburg and the center of government. After all, it was time for Pennsylvania to do what New York had done in moving its seat of government to Albany, and Virginia had done in moving its seat to Richmond. It was time for Pennsylvania's government to move in the direction of the people: west.

Harris Jr. began meeting with his son-in-law William McClay to lay out the town of Harrisburg as early as 1784. They began with the development of a county. Harris Jr. was tired of doing all of his business transactions in the city of Lancaster, which was the seat of Lancaster County. It was time for a new county to be carved out of the existing Lancaster County. They began developing the boundaries of the new county as they also considered a name. Together they chose "Dauphin County." *Dauphin* is the title given to the son of the king of France. This would be a sign of appreciation to France for its assistance during the Revolutionary War. Without French munitions, uniforms, food, troops, and naval presence, the war could not have been won.

Harris Jr. and McClay submitted the proposal to the Assembly in Philadelphia for debate. And debate, they did. The issues centered around Harris Jr's plan to carve out a profitable section of Lancaster County, and by doing so, bankrupt what remained of Lancaster County. Harris Jr. was seen by legislators from Lancaster as a radical and even crazy and egotistical. They argued that anyone in his right mind could never vote in favor of that plan and watch their fellow citizens plunged into financial ruin. To say it got ugly was mild. In an article dated February 1785 in *Freedman's Journal*, Harris Jr. and McClay are called every name in the book in hopes of making them look inept at presenting a well-thought-out plan. But they had presented a well-thought-out plan, and the proposal went before the Assembly for a vote on March 4, 1785. On that day, the Pennsylvania Assembly voted to separate Dauphin County from Lancaster County and make Harris' Ferry its county seat. Harris Jr. and McClay were victorious.

The first thing Harris Jr. went about doing was donating land and money for the building of a courthouse, a jail, a prison, and a pillory. The courthouse was located on the corner of Front and Washington Streets. The pillory was about sixty yards south of Harris Sr's grave, just north of the ferry launch.

Harris Jr. then offered up some of his own land (four acres and twenty-one perches) for the county seat, which is where the capital building sits today. Then he donated land to the Salem Reformed Congregation for the first church within Harris' Ferry. Harris Jr. sat down with McClay and began to draw a map of the town into parcels. He'd had this planned since March 3, 1784. He had high ground above his mansion divided into two hundred one-quarter–acre lots, intersected by streets, lanes, and alleys. Harris Jr. would keep twenty of the lots for himself.

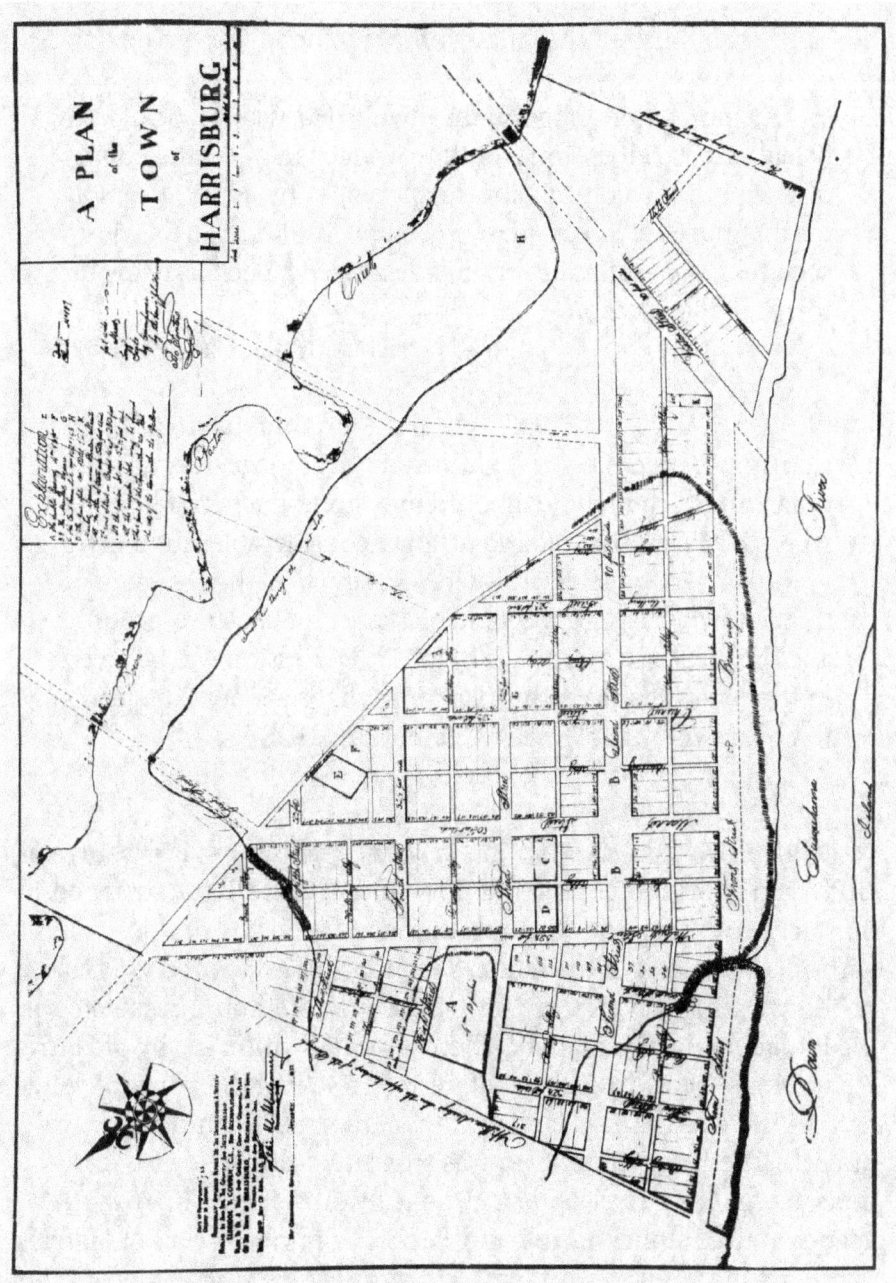

A plan for the city of Harrisburg, drawn by John Harris Jr. and William McClay.

The June 4, 1785, edition of *Freedman's Journal*, (one of several newspapers published in Philadelphia) included these two articles:

The purchasers of lots in the town of Harrisburgh [sic] lately laid out at Harris' ferry on the Susquehanna, in the county of Dauphin, by commissioners appointed by act of assembly for that purpose, are requested to apply to John Harris within six weeks from this date for their deeds, which he has ready for them at that place.

—Harrisburgh, [sic] June 4, 1785

To be SOLD or LET, A Large and commodious stone-mansion house, two stories high, fifty by forty feet deep, with a cellar under the whole, and a large stone-kitchen adjoining where a tavern has been kept for a considerable number of years past—completely finished, and situate in the above mentioned town; having garden, stables, meadow, pasture-ground, and orchard, and a good well, &c. &c. Possession will be given in three months from this date or perhaps sooner. The terms to be known by applying to JOHN HARRRIS

—June 4, 1785

Notice two things: First, the original spelling of Harrisburg included an *h* on the end. While it would eventually be dropped in most cities except for Pittsburgh, Harrisburg had its beginnings with a *h* on the end of the name. Second, Harris Jr. was trying to sell his house. This was not the only time that the house was listed in the Philadelphia newspapers. There is no indication in any of Harris Jr.'s writings as to why he was interested in selling the house. A letter dated 1780 shows that Harris Jr. was no longer running the tavern himself. The letter of petition was submitted for "a license to run a house of publick [sic] entertainment by Abraham Murrow—Innkeeper at the Publick house and Ferry (Commonly Called Harris's Ferry).[62] One is left to wonder if Harris Jr. was getting weary of all of

---

62 "Letter from Abraham Murrow to the justices of the peace, August 4, 1780," Lancaster County Historical Society.

the work and challenges, or if he was busy with his other endeavors and needed to unload his very big house. We are left to speculate why he would want to sell such a mansion.

It was at this time that Harris Jr. founded what would become the Harrisburg Academy. In 1785, he began the work of educating children in that frontier town, because he believed that education would make a difference in the long run for the people of Harris' Ferry. Within one year, Harris Jr. had a list of eighty-four people willing to contribute funds or supplies to the academy, along with a board of directors to which he could hand over the academy's operation.

In 1785, tax rolls show that there were close to two thousand persons living in what is now the greater Harrisburg area, which extends from the foot of Peter's Mountain to Middletown to Hanover Township. One hundred and forty-three names were recorded on the tax record for Harrisburg. With family members added in, the population totaled six hundred in the town proper.[63] By 1787, there were six professional carpenters, five blacksmiths, five joiners, three doctors, and four shoemakers, as well as wheelwrights, saddlers, millwrights, distillers, brewers, plasterers, stonemasons, a silversmith, tailors, weavers, brickmakers, storekeepers, tanners, and painters.[64]

According to the writings of his son, Robert, the state Assembly entrusted Harris Jr. with the privilege of naming the town. He chose the name *Harrisburgh*. His choice sparked a five-year battle with Chief Justice Thomas McKean,[65] who chose to show some petty spite he held for John Harris Jr. by forcing the Assembly to adopt the name *Louisburg*, after Louis XVI of France, since the county was being named after his oldest son (Dauphin). McKean and Harris Jr. did not like each other, and this was McKean's way of putting Harris Jr. in his place. We are not given the reason for the dispute between Harris Jr. and McKean in any of their writings, but the animosity is mentioned by others. McKean was chief justice, and he previously lived in Harris' Ferry. It is possible that he believed that he was not

---

63 Luther R. Kelker, *History of Dauphin County*, 498–500.
64 Ibid.
65 George H. Morgan, *Centennial*, 209.

being given the respect he was due. Harris Jr. owned the land, and he held fast as the Assembly went back and forth on the name. His final statement, which settled the issue, was, "You may call it Louisburg all you please but I'll not sell an inch more of land unless the town's to be named Harrisburg."[66] In all my research, there is no place where Harris Jr. refers to the future name of the town as anything other than *Harrisburg*. The resolution was not finalized until April 13, 1791, when the town was established as a borough by the state Assembly.

Harris Jr. set aside 6.22 acres along the river front for a landing and a street that would run along the riverfront for the public good. The tract included his father's grave and the ferry landing, where Paxton Street ended at the Susquehanna River. All evidence of the ferry landing was destroyed with the building of the railroad bridge some years later. On the eastern shore, people came down Paxton Street and stepped right onto the ferryboat. The ferry traveled just below the big island (modern-day City Island) and landed on the west shore at the location of the hard turn in the turnpike (known as "the bottleneck" today). No evidence of the west shore landing of Harris' ferry is present today. There was a tollhouse on the western shore, but it is long gone. The ferry utilized the river's current and socket poles. It was also common for a rope to extend from one side of the river to the other to make navigation as easy as possible.

There are accounts of mules being used to pull unusually large loads, with the help of pulley systems. The mules stayed on the shore while the ferry was connected to the rope and pulley system. The mules would march off in one direction, and the ferry would move across the river. While it was possible for Harris Jr. to have used such a system, we have no written record of it. As far as we know, Harris Jr. had a small fleet (exactly how many, we don't know) of flat-bottom boats capable of ferrying heavy cargo across the river. The ferry could handle Conestoga wagons, horses, cannon, baggage, pack horses, and more. The cost was minimal and was most likely in the shillings and pence

---

66 Luther R. Kelker, *History of Dauphin County*, 499.

range, not pounds. The pillory was located near the boat launch and publick [sic] house, possibly to keep people from getting out of hand while waiting for the ferry. Depending on the conditions on the Susquehanna, a person or family could wait hours or days—even weeks. The flood of 1786 would have kept people from crossing by ferry for quite a long time. Ferry crossings were at the mercy of the water level and weather conditions. Travelers could set up a makeshift camp, or they could stay in Harris Jr.'s publick house for a small fee.

From 1785 through 1787, Harris Jr. worked to make Harrisburg the town people would want to live in. The town remained on the frontier of Pennsylvania, where bear wandered into town and Harris Jr. shot turkeys from the door of his storehouse.[67] Deer, otter, beaver, elk, and the occasional bison were all part of this new and growing town. The river itself was teeming with all kinds of fish and wildlife, and the yearly shad run provided barrels and barrels of salted fish that would see people through the winter. That same river would provide thick blocks of ice that would keep storage houses cool into June. Fowl of all kinds filled the sky and provided excellent eating.

Harris Jr.'s advertisements in the Philadelphia papers would attract young men looking for opportunities to branch out on their own and set up a shop in a new town that needed services of all kinds. Journeymen from Philadelphia could launch in Harrisburg and become masters of their trades with little to no competition and a market that could sustain a good life. A person could relocate to Harrisburg and rent a small place or even buy a plot of land and establish himself as a tradesman. In no time, the town went from 143 plot owners to 200. Harris had found a niche that Reading or Lancaster could not compete in, and people were beginning to see Harrisburg as the place that Harris Jr. believed it could be.

And then tragedy struck Harris Jr. again—twice. In 1785, he and Mary lost a grandson, who had been born to his daughter Mary and William McClay. Two years later, Harris Jr.'s heart was struck with the same pain he had experienced some twenty years before. Mary,

---

67 Luther R. Kelker, *History of Dauphin County*, vol. 2, 502.

his wife of twenty-three years, fell sick and died on November 1, 1787. As with his first wife, Elizabeth, we are left with no cause of death for Mary Reed Harris. John wrote nothing about her passing, and I have not been able to find anything written by her surviving children. As much as Robert Harris and Mary Harris Hanna wrote, one would think they would have written something about her death. It leads me to believe that either it was not fashionable to write about a mother's passing, or the deaths left them "speechless."

Harris Jr. buried Mary with Elizabeth at the Paxton Presbyterian Church graveyard, where he had been a member of the congregation for most of his life. He would eventually lie down with both of them for his own eternal rest. Losing Mary must have been a heavy pain to bear. He had lost the love of his youth, and now he had lost the partner who had walked alongside him as he made a name for himself. It was somewhere during this period that his youngest brother, David, died while on a voyage to Europe. The cause of death for David was not given.

I was able to find a document at the Pennsylvania Historical Society dated 1787 and showing that Harris Jr. hired a man named Rory Fraizer to accomplish a long list of tasks that would be considered hard labor. The list included things like "drawing logs from out of the river, setting post and rail fence, assisting the stone masons, digging a drain, digging a foundation, digging a cellar, and chinking and daubing two houses." All of these things were back-breaking work, and I wonder if Frazier was a young man trying to get his start. Or possibly, he owed Harris Jr. some money, so Harris Jr. gave him the hardest jobs to do. The document is a record of the labor and the value to be paid to the laborer, coming to a total of £19 5s. 11d. The notation at the bottom of the bill is "Harriss-Burgh Decber An 1787." This work was not only difficult, but it was also done in December, which can be a cold and nasty time of year, especially to pull logs out of the river and to dig foundations and cellars.

The following year, 1788, John Penn, son of William Penn, journeyed from Philadelphia to Carlisle. He stopped in Harrisburg and noted his stay "at Harrisburg or Harris' Ferry." He referred to John Harris Jr. as the owner and founder of the town and comments that it is "one of the finest I ever saw."[68] Penn mentions the home known as "Compass House" as one of the first public houses in Pennsylvania. There is no mention of Harris Jr. being a widower, which I find interesting, since travelers tend to write down tidbits of interest that would have been common knowledge to everyone. So, the idea that common knowledge keeps persons from writing down significant information is ruled out, since other commonly known information is written about, such as the width of the river being three-quarters of a mile.

It was during these tumultuous and busy days in the life of Harris Jr. that the United States Constitution was written and suggestions for a national leader were being put forward. Harris Jr. was a fan of George Washington, like so many other Americans in his day, and most likely saw Washington as the most appropriate choice to fill this new position of president. His correspondence with Washington during the French and Indian War had spurred his lifelong admiration of Washington. As a politician, Harris Jr. pushed for his friends and family members to be involved in politics, and he believed that everyone should serve for at least one term in some form of government. His son-in-law, William McClay, was the first senator to serve under the new government, and his son, David, was politically connected for the entirety of his life. Correspondence between McClay and Washington can be found in Washington's papers and gives evidence that both McClay and David Harris were well-known in political circles.

The first census of the United States reveals some interesting things about the surrounding counties, as well as about John Harris Jr. In the 1790 census, there are a total of 184 male, tax-paying, landowners listed by name, living in "Harrisburgh"—notice the *h* is still on the end. The breakdown of those who were living in each household is as follows: free White males of sixteen years and upward, including heads of families; free White males under sixteen years; free White females, including heads of families; and slaves. John Harris Jr.'s name appears first on the list for his household,

---

68 Luther R. Kelker, *History of Dauphin County,* 501.

which includes three White males of sixteen years of age or more, two White males under sixteen, seven White females, and six slaves, for a total of twelve Whites and six enslaved Black persons. The three males over sixteen included Harris Jr. himself; his debilitated son, Johnny; and we can only guess that it also included Robert, who was said to be living in the old log house. At this point in 1790, Robert was married, but they had yet to have any of the seven children they would birth, so none of the children listed in the census is theirs. Johnny never married or had children, so none of the women or children are connected to him. One of the two White males under sixteen would have been Harris Jr.'s youngest son, James, who was all of eight years old in 1790. The fact that there are seven other White people listed leads me to believe that there were other persons living on the Harris Jr. property. It could be that the Harrisburg Academy was housing children on the property. That could account for the other White males under sixteen and the seven other females (inclusive of heads of households, which would have included Robert's wife, Elizabeth). Harris Jr. was fully supporting eighteen people who were living on his property in Harrisburg in 1790. A combination of the census and the weight of caring for so many lives may have driven him to write out his last will and testament that year.

His will was a full eight pages long and incredibly thorough. He included the disposition of large tracts of land on both sides of the Susquehanna, the house he built, the outbuildings, the ferry, many of the family treasures, and human beings. He cared for each of his family members, but especially Johnny, who was unable to care for himself, and James, who was just too young to do so. He also listed each of the enslaved people and how they were to be cared for once he died. I comfortably estimate that his estate would be worth millions today. The inventory of the estate included a vast number of items, including farm goods and implements, a sleigh, queenswear, pewter, glass, books, coffee and a coffee mill, sheets and comforters, horses, guns, and the list goes on. Many of the things in the inventory were sold—not to pay off debts but to add to the cash on hand for the estate. Harris Jr.'s will set aside large amounts of money for the care of people, the start of the Harrisburg Academy, and the future of the city of Harrisburg. Some of those funds would go directly to the perpetual care and release of the enslaved people at the Harris plantation. It is time we take a deeper look at enslaved life at Compass House under John Harris Jr.

Chapter 8

JOHN HARRIS JR. AND SERVITUDE

The issue of slavery in Pennsylvania and specifically in the life of the Harris family is one we need to look at headlong. John Harris Sr. was reported to have had four servants at Paxton. We know them by name because they were recorded for us. They were Tom, Cherida, her child, and Hercules. As far as we know, none of them were transferred to John Harris Jr. At least there is no record that any of them were passed on when Harris Sr. died in 1748 at what we believe was the age of seventy-five. It is possible that they went with Esther Harris, the widow of Harris Sr., when she remarried. It was common for the widow to claim ownership of both possessions and people, as terrible as that sounds.

We know, through stories that were passed down, that Hercules was given his freedom as a reward for recusing Harris Sr. from a band of Native Americans who, when not satisfied with enough rum, decided to burn Harris Sr. to death. The story was told primarily by Robert Harris, a grandson of Harris Sr. (one of Harris Jr.'s children with Mary). There is no documentation of Harris Jr. telling the story, maybe because he was not there in person. The event is supposed to have happened in either 1718 or 1719—eight or nine years before Harris Jr. was born—according to William H. Egle.[69] The Provincial Records have no documentation of this event, which is surprising, if it is in fact true. The mulberry tree to which the Native Americans tied Harris Sr. in order to burn him was the same tree that he was buried beneath. It is also said that Hercules was buried with him as a sign of the closeness of their relationship. There is no substantial evidence, such as that produced by ground-penetrating radar, that Hercules was buried beside his friend, John Harris Sr. The story of Harris Sr.'s rescue by Hercules is told in every historical record of the founding of Harrisburg that I could find.

The story of Hercules heroically coming the aid of his master is unique to the time period. Admittedly, it is completely within the realm of possibility that Hercules was looking out for his own interests. If his master was tortured and killed, where would that leave Hercules and the other Blacks who were enslaved at Harris Sr.'s homestead? Previous accounts would suggest that the people who remained at Harris Sr.'s homestead could have been taken into captivity by the Native Americans and forced to become a part of the tribal life. Sometimes a singular captive was chosen to die by torture as a way to appease the anger of the tribe. Hercules would have been familiar with those kinds of stories and may have been afraid for his life and the lives of others at Harris Sr.'s homestead. His life would have gone from uncomfortable to unbearable. So it would be better to save Harris Sr. and keep what was known, than to see Harris Sr. die and risk everything.

As Harris Jr. established himself on the Susquehanna, we discover that a list of the names of "servants" begins to appear. As I mentioned previously, none of the names of Harris Sr.'s slaves appear in Harris Jr.'s records. That does not mean they were not transferred to him; it just means that records of the transfer of those persons have not been uncovered to date. By the time we get to 1780, though, we have a clear record of those who were

---

69 George H. Morgan, *Centennial*, 182.

held in servitude at Harris' Ferry under the ownership of John Harris Jr. and his wife, Mary. The Gradual Abolition Act of March 1780 required that all Negro and mulatto, slaves and servants had to be registered with the state's Provincial Assembly by November 1.

Register of Negro and
Mullatto Slaves
and Servants
1780

The registry mandated by Pennsylvania's Provincial Assembly in 1780.

This registry is kept at the Lancaster County Historical Society library, and when my wife and I turned its pages, we saw the listings of persons in the state of Pennsylvania who lived in some form of servitude. We were fortunate to find the page where John Harris Jr. and his wife Mary's enslaved persons were recorded. On October 9, 1780, there is the record of six people who are under the ownership of "John Harris of Paxton Twp, Yeoman, and Mary Reed of Paxton

§ 1 negroe woman named Juddy aged about 20 years for life

James McKee of Paxtang twp., enters as owner
1 negroe woman named Hannah aged about 25 yrs. Slave for life
1 Mulato Girl named Paulina aged 3 yrs. as slave
1 Mulato Boy named George aged 6 months. as slave

Oct 9) John Harris of Paxtang Twp. Yeoman, enters as owner

1 negroe man named Jack aged 48 years
1 negroe boy named Isaac aged 16 years last August.
1 negroe boy named Frank aged 14 years last May

Mary Reed of Paxtang Twp, widow, enters as owner
1 negroe woman named Dinah aged 27 years
1 Molata, her daughter named Nancy, 9 yrs. last November
1 negroe child named Jack aged one month.

1780) Oct 9) Robert Spear of Hempfield Twp. enters as his property
1 negroe man named George aged 35 years.
1 Mullato man named James Richards aged about 26 years.
1 Negroe woman named Debe aged about 29 years
1 negroe Girl named Rose aged about 10 years
1 Mulato Girl named Phulas aged about 7 years
1 Mullato Girl named Charity aged about 5 years
1 Negroe Girl named Adah aged about 3 years
1 Negroe Girl named Sidney aged about 1 year

Harris Jr.'s slaves, as of 1780.

Twp, widow" The list included:

1 negroe man named Jack aged 48 years
1 negroe boy named Isaac aged 16 years last August
1 negroe boy named Frank aged 14 years last May
1 negroe woman named Dinah aged 27 years
1 Mulata, her daughter named Nancy 9 yrs. last November
1 negroe child named Jack aged one month[70]

There is a bit of a discrepancy in the list, which happens over the years. It appears that an individual named Frank is claimed to be a "slave" of John Harris Jr., but the records don't line up. An article in the *National Gazette* of Philadelphia from November 11, 1839, states that

Frank died on November 8, 1839, and was born in "about 1745, where Harrisburg now stands" making him ninety-four years old. While attaining that age is not impossible, it is a bit improbable. Life expectancy in the eighteenth and early nineteenth centuries was not much beyond forty-five or fifty years for a healthy, White, landowner, who was well fed and had access (albeit limited) to medicine. To suggest that a slave would live to ninety-four was almost unheard of. Harris Jr.'s slave Jack is referred to as "Old Jack" in Harris Jr.'s last will and testament. Jack would have been fifty-nine years old in 1791, and that was considered old.

There is a slave named Frank owned by Harris Jr., who is listed in the 1780 record. He was fourteen years old in 1780, meaning he was born in 1766. He would have been twenty-five years old in 1791, when Harris Jr. passed away and seventy-three years old in 1839—a much more likely age for a man who most likely worked very hard all of his life. The last will and testament of John Harris Jr. does not list Frank as a part of the goods and persons that he bequeaths to his family. The article from 1839 states that Frank was manumitted by the late Mr. Adam Orth of Newmarket Forge, in Lebanon (then Dauphin) County. I cannot be absolutely sure that these references are to the same person. There are several possibilities. First, it is possible that the dates are believed to be

---

70 *Register of Negro and Mullatto Slaves and Servants*, Lancaster County Historical Society library, Lancaster, Pennsylvania.

correct, but they are not. I find it hard to believe that Harris Jr. would have noted Frank's age incorrectly in a formal and official document of the Pennsylvania government. In every way, John Harris Jr. was a man of integrity, so I am led to believe that the Frank whom he lists is in fact the fourteen-year-old listed in the 1780 record book.

Second, Frank could have fabricated or embellished the story a bit for his own purposes. Since records were not well kept and people did not do a great deal of research into someone's story, it is possible that Frank was fudging the numbers. Third, it is possible that Frank didn't know just how old he was and came up with an age based on his personal experiences and to the best of his ability. I'd like to give Frank the benefit of the doubt and believe that the Frank in the article is the same person who is listed in the 1780 record of slaves in Pennsylvania. Herein lies the problem of tracking down reliable records to get the best understanding of what was happening at the Harris plantation—or on the property of any other landowner who owned slaves or had indentures in Paxton.

Research into the life and history of people of color in America is challenging since many people like Frank never took on a surname. Some servants were in the practice of adopting their owner's last name. But Frank did not take on the name "Harris." Records suggest that none of the enslaved persons at the Harris plantation, including the famous Hercules, took on the surname of Harris. If they did, which is not out of the question, the records do not show it. This fact has made it impossible to locate Hercules's grave to this very day.

Herein lies the trouble that is inherent in the historical research of African Americans. How people were treated, and the systems in place that maintained that treatment, kept persons of color from living full and free lives. The complications are compounded by those owners who had no morals or scruples. They were committed to keeping certain races of people in such a downcast condition that there was little to no hope to be found outside of that offered through faith and hope in the eternal freedom offered by God in heaven. The 1839 *National Gazette* article says that Frank often went to church (Paxton Presbyterian on Progress Avenue) to worship with the Harris family.

REPORTS that Rev. Sterling M. Means, 628 Herr street, Harrisburg, leading historian of the Negro race in America, may come to Altoona to deliver talks before service clubs, churches and lodges, draws attention to the efforts to locate the grave of Frank, once slave of John Harris, Jr., founder of Gov. Martin's beautiful Capital city, who passed away on Nov. 8, 1839; in speaking of his demise the National Gazette of Nov. 11, 1839, Philadelphia, says:

"HARRISBURG. — Died, in the Dauphin county home, Saturday last, Frank, formerly a slave of Mr. John Harris, the founder of Harrisburg, Pa. He was born about 1745, where Harrisburg now stands, and was almost or more than ninety years of age at the time of his death, He was manumitted by the late Mr. Adam Orth, of "Newmarket Forge," in Lebanon (then Dauphin) county. Frank remembered when the Indian smoked his pipe and when the forest covered what is now the site of Harrisburg. He used to say he had 'turned many a furrow between the Canal and the bridge across the river.' He also said that he had often played and wrestled with James Logan, the Mingo chief, then a young man. Frank also liked to tell of accompanying his master and family to Paztang Church, he and another servant armed, as well as Mr. Harris—of the weapons stacked and scattered around the Church.

"JOHN Elder, the clergyman was a Colonel in the Militia, and displayed courage on many a trying occasion." •

NEGRO fraternal organizations are trying to locate the grave and get Don Cadzow's historical commission to put up a state marker. Many have wondered if Frank was the slave who brought the friendly Indians to the aid of John Harris, Sr., when tied to the old mulberry tree on Front street, Harrisburg, and like Col. Crawford, to be burned at the stake, only not a friendly hand was raised to save Crawford, even though several of the white race, including Col. Simon Girty (Gerdes), were present at this awful outburst of the redskins' fury, but the senior Harris' deliverer was named Hercules.

An 1839 obituary for a man who may have been owned by the Harris family.

So, recognizing these complexities and being willing to wrestle with the truths of our past has allowed us to dive into historical records and find more today than ever before. Let's look at those persons of color, both "Negroe" and "Mullattoe," who found themselves in the ownership of John and Mary Reed Harris. As a point of reference, I am using the terms that were in common use (and the spelling of those terms) because I am striving to be as historically accurate as possible. While these are terms we do not use today and some may find offensive, they were commonly used in the days of John Harris Jr.

Here's what I have discovered. There are six persons listed in October 1780 in the Record of Slave, Servants, Negroes and Mullattoes in Pennsylvania. The Gradual Abolition Act of Slavery was voted on in March 1780 and required that all enslaved persons be registered with the state by November 1 of that year. As a member of the Assembly, Harris Jr. naturally complied. The act was first presented to the Assembly on August 21, 1778. But Congress was dealing with war matters and did not have time for the Abolition Act. Abolitionists like George Bryan brought the issue before the Assembly again in 1779 with a special focus on children born into slavery. Previously, a child was a slave based on the position of his/her mother. If the mother was a slave, then the child was automatically a slave by law.

The final decision would wait until March 1, 1780, when the Gradual Abolition Act was read to the Congress. There were fourteen sections within the act, addressing different and sundry elements of the slave issue in Pennsylvania. The first dealt with the hypocrisy of a nation so blessed by God with what looked like an imminent triumph over the tyranny of Great Britain that could continue to maintain a tyrannical position over a race of people. The argument was that since God had extended a hand of freedom to the United States, these states should do the same for "all men (who) are created equal."

The final wording of the act said this: Anyone born after the act was signed on March 1, 1780, was to remain a "servant" under the current master and then be released into freedom on or before his or her twenty-eighth birthday. Those who were slaves before the act was signed were to remain as slaves unless their masters chose to release them. The act abolished the importation of slaves to Pennsylvania and stated that non-Pennsylvanians residing in the state had to comply with the act within six months of residency in the commonwealth. Congressmen (and even President Washington) had to deal with this, as they served in Philadelphia by rotating their slaves out of Pennsylvania every six months.

"An Act for the Gradual Abolition of Slavery" was passed by the Assembly on March 1, 1780, making Pennsylvania the first state to phase out slavery.

The act would be amended in positive ways in 1788. Two additional aspects of slavery were addressed in the amendments. First, it was now forbidden for a slaveholder to transport a pregnant slave across a border to avoid obeying the act by having the child born into slavery in another state that did not have the same rules in place. Secondly, it was now the law that persons who owned enslaved individuals and were relocating to Pennsylvania were required to set those persons free upon moving into the state permanently.

Harris Jr.'s list in 1780 was made up of four males and two females, one of the females being *mulata* or mixed race. This status was common enough that it was listed as a category in the title of the record book. Her name was Nancy, and she was the daughter of Monah Dinah. And yes, we could choose to go down the rabbit hole of the parentage of Nancy. We unfortunately do not have any known descendants of Nancy with whom we can converse or who might provide DNA in an effort to discover who Nancy's father might have been. As the first-person interpreter of Harris Jr., I would like to think that he didn't have that kind of tendency, and therefore Nancy's father must have been someone else. There surely were plenty of opportunities with White males other than John Harris Jr. I by no means wish to cast an ill light on Monah Dinah. In every way, she must have been an exceptional woman based on how Harris Jr. cared for her in his will.

Let us take a look at the desires of Harris Jr. toward each of his "servants," according to his final will. The last will and testament of John Harris Jr. is eight pages long, and each page is 11 inches by 17 inches. He cared for a great number of details in the will, including the future situation of each of his servants or *negroe(s)* as he notates. The first person he cares for is found on page six. Here's what the will says:

> *I give and bequeath to my son David Harris, my negroe man Isaac, to serve him my said son David, for an during the term of ten years, for the time of my decease, and at the expiration of said term I direct that my said negroe be set free, as a reward for his fidelity.*

David is John's third-oldest child from his marriage to Elizabeth. He is well established by 1790, when the will is written. So Harris Jr. trusts him, and the will suggests that Isaac is well thought of by Harris Jr. Isaac was twenty-six years old in 1790.

The next servants to be cared for are found in the very next paragraph. It says:

> *I give and bequeath to my daughter Mary Hannah my negroe Monah Dinah and her child Nancy and said Nanse's child named [the space is blank] and in order that she my said daughter Mary may remember her father when he is moldering*

into dust, and this his last injunction of care and attention as well to the preservation of the morals as the improvement of the mind of her Orphan and infant brother James, I give and devise to her my said daughter my long silver soup and table spoons and also all my tea spoons.

It is to be assumed from this that John has given the females and what might be an infant or young child to his daughter Mary. She was to use the proceeds from the very expensive silverware to care for them and for James, her younger brother. The honor given to Mary was that she received the largest number of persons to care for—three servants and James. Nancy was nineteen, and this child's grandmother, Dinah, was now thirty-seven.

The next notation is in the next paragraph on page six. It reads:

I give and bequeath to my son Robert Harris my Negroe boy young Jack, the feather bed, bedstead and furniture where on he now sleeps and also my silver Pint.

Jack was one month old in October 1780, making him ten years old in 1790 when the will was drawn up. Jack was to keep the bed and all its bedding and the furniture, such as a chest of drawers. In another 18 years he would be a free man, based on being born after the act abolishing slavery was passed.

The next person to be cared for is found at the top of page seven. I reads like this:

It is my will and I do hereby order and direct that my old Negroe man Jack be supported during life by my son Robert Harris and my Daughter Mary Hannah at their joint and equal expense, but in case he should become so troublesome as to require to be confined, I then direct that he be supported by my executor during life, out of my estate generally.

It is my assumption from the wording used here that "Old Jack" was not in good health. At the time the will was written in 1790, he was fifty-eight years old and had undoubtedly worked hard all his life. Life on the frontier was hard and made even more challenging for slaves. I can only imagine that Old Jack had seen a few things in his lifetime. If these dates are in fact correct, he would have been born in 1732. He is not listed under the ownership of Harris Sr., so we are left to assume that Harris Jr. acquired him sometime after his father died in 1748. By 1790, it was obvious to Harris Jr. that Jack was not well and would need care. He gave the task to the brother and sister, Robert and Mary, and states clearly that whatever the cost, it will come out of their pockets. Both of them grew up with Old Jack. Now it was their job to take care of him. And if he were to get so infirmed as to need "confinement," the estate would pay for it. No matter what happened to Old Jack in the years to come, he was to be cared for—whatever the cost.

Six enslaved persons are recorded in the 1790 census as owned by John Harris Jr. One thing I noticed was that Frank's name was not in the will. It is my thought that he had been sold or traded sometime between the 1780 recording and the 1790 census, quite possibly to Mr. Adam Orth, who gave him his freedom. This is one of the difficult things about slavery that I wrestle with. Did something happen that made Frank, who was fourteen in 1780, no longer desirable to Harris Jr.? Was there no longer a need for a fourth man? Did Frank do something wrong and by doing so, force Harris Jr. to sell or trade him? Or perhaps Frank had family connections with another owner, and it was humane to sell him so he could be with his relatives. Or maybe Frank ran away, and Harris Jr. moved on and did not try to get him back. I would love to know, but as of now, the trail is difficult to track. I hope that one day I will have an answer to the questions I've raised here about Frank.

I can, in no way, give John Harris Jr. or his family a free pass when it comes to slavery. It is clear that they owned people, human beings. William McClay and John Andre Hanna—Harris Jr.'s two sons-in law, owned people. Several good friends of Harris Jr. are listed as owning slaves in the 1790 census. And while the institution of slavery that existed in the eighteenth century was complex and convoluted, so much so that we will never be able to fully understand it as we look backward, we must still challenge the thought process of those slave owners. It is my understanding from all my research that Harris Jr. was kind and generous to those he owned and that he educated each one so that they could function at the top of their craft. At the end of the day, though, they were still his property. I am comforted by the knowledge that Harris Jr. was a part of passing the Gradual Abolition Act of Slavery in Pennsylvania, the first state to do so.

I am glad to see that Harris Jr. identified each person by name in his will and instructed how they were to be cared for as a way to show their importance and significance in his life. His sensitivity to Old Jack's health (mental or physical) is a sign that he paid attention to the well-being of each person because he saw them as people. He lived out his everyday life with Jack, Isaac, Monah Dinah, Nancy (and child), and young Jack by his side. It is my hope that they were like family to him and that there was a mutual respect and, dare I say it, affection for each other that grew over the years at Compass House on the Harris plantation.

Chapter 9

HIS LEGACY

In 1791, John Harris Jr. was about to turn sixty-five years old, and he had accomplished great things. The nation he lived in had gone through the process of creating a brand-new constitution, and the first president of the United States, George Washington, was seated. These things had never been done before, and John Harris Jr. was an active participant in the creation of a sovereign nation. Harris Jr.'s legacy includes taking over his father's business, serving during the French and Indian War as a militia captain, and supplying the war effort during the American Revolution. It included the founding of Dauphin County, naming the county seat Harrisburg after his father, John Harris Sr., and serving in government. He donated the land for the Harrisburg courthouse, the jail, riverfront park, and for a congregation to build a church on the corner of Third Street and Cherry Alley. He was generous, kind, and giving. One description of him reads:

> John Harris was described as tall, well-proportioned and sturdy man, with good teeth, a smooth shaven and healthy appearance, and hair inclined to turn gray from an original rich brown. This he wore in the fashion of his time, and upon the Fourth of July had it powdered. His dress was "leather

breeches," in the fit of which he took great-pride; brown coat and vest, long white woolen stocking, silver buckles and heavy, low-cut shoes. He was found of his gun, rod and dog, and equally fond of fishing or of a shooting match; quite adept at "long bullets," or shuffleboards. He did not hesitate about expressing an opinion upon any subject of discussion, and was most emphatic in his admiration of George Washington and those who served under him.[71]

He was successful by any standard set in the eighteenth century, but he was now alone. His first wife, Elizabeth, had been gone for twenty-seven years. His second wife, Mary, had been gone for four years. While he was surrounded by grown children, grandchildren, two brothers, nieces and nephews, and a community that adored and respected him, he was without a life partner. This did not stop him from continuing to do good things and to be as much of a man of honor as possible. Once again, I want to quote his obituary in the August 4, 1791, edition of the Philadelphia *Freeman's Journal*:

> He was charitable to the poor, compassionate to the afflicted, and lenitive to those over whom he had power. As a citizen, he was active, and useful; as a husband, parent and master, he was tender, kind and indulgent: beloved in his lifetime by most, lamented in his death by all.

Harris was in the twilight of his life, and evidence shows us that he was keenly aware of his position. He had made out his last will and testament in 1790. We don't know what precipitated him doing so. His obituary states that he was "without experiencing a day's sickness; except with the small-pox or measles."

In the spring of 1791, two wonderful things happened for John Harris Jr. On May 12, his son Robert was married in Philadelphia to Miss Elizabeth Ewing, the daughter of Rev. John Ewing D.D., the provost of the University of Pennsylvania. That same spring, the

---

71 Harris McIntosh, *A Chronicle of the Harris and McIntosh Families*, 1980, 45.

argument over the name of the county seat was resolved by an act of the State Assembly, which voted, finally, to call the town *Harris-burg*. Harris Jr. owned close to two thousand acres on both sides of the Susquehanna River, both north and south of Harrisburg. Being a man of vision, it was clear as early as 1789 that Harris Jr. and Senator McClay (his son-in-law) dreamed of Harrisburg becoming the seat of government for the entire state of Pennsylvania.[72] Harris was ever looking forward to those things that could be.

His work in 1786 had also managed to pull together an influential group of men who were able to begin what would be an educational institution, giving children a chance to learn and grow. Their statement of loyalty is admirable. It reads:

> We, the subscribers, do each of us for ourselves promise to pay, or cause to be paid, to John Hoge, Moses Gilmor, Conrad Bombaugh and John Brooks, or their order upon demand, the sums annexed to each of our names respectively, to be applied by them in purchasing materials for an in building a schoolhouse in one corner of the public ground in the town of Harrisburg.[73]

The school, known as Harrisburg Academy, was to be open to English and German students and for the general education of all. Harris writes in his will that the proceeds from his ferry are to be used, if the state allows, for the support of the school in perpetuity. And while the school would not remain in Harris Jr.'s house or on the east shore of the Susquehanna all of its life, it does still exist to this very day. Harris Jr.'s ability to gather people around him and in so doing, accomplish great things lasted his entire life.

On what was surely a hot and humid central Pennsylvania day, on July 29, 1791, John Harris Jr. closed his eyes to this life for the final time. We do not have a cause of death. The possibilities are too vast to even speculate. He may have been sick for some time, which caused him to make out his will in 1790. It may have been

---

72Carl Lamson Carmer, *The Susquehanna*, 198.
73 George H. Morgan, *Centennial*, 92.

something sudden and catastrophic that took him out of this world. Medical science, being what it was in 1791, did not provide us with a postmortem examination, letting us know the cause of his demise. All we know is, he was dead, and the loss was felt by many people across Pennsylvania.

His life had spanned the period from 1727 to 1791, including the violent convulsing of a land that would give birth to a new nation called the United States of America. He fought in a war, and he gave as much or more of his blood, sweat, and tears to the development of what would become the town of Harrisburg. He amassed a large fortune and a great many personal and plantation possessions.

Over the following months and years, the will was probated. Most of his possessions were either sold or allocated to those to whom they were promised. The inventory of his possessions, six pages long, is currently under the care of the Pennsylvania Historical Society in Philadelphia. He owned everything from tons of wheat and other grains to horses, multiple wagons, a sleigh, and prized family heirlooms, such as silver spoons and a silver tea set. The inventory tells its own story. Not only was John Harris Jr. wealthy, but he was a man of means who enjoyed the finer things in life. Yes, he had enough pewter dishes to serve and feed a small army. But he also had queenswear, a type of light, white earthenware with a unique glaze and paten, and creamware imported from England—enough to offer fine dining to twenty to twenty-five persons. He had sheets and blankets aplenty, as well as beds and other furniture. *Mahogany* is one of the words that stands out when reading the list of chairs and dining table. It is impressive to see the number of fine wares and linens that he possessed. While he loved his frontier, he was, indeed, a man of wealth and possessions. While there is not a tally of his total wealth, there is no doubt he was, by modern standards, nothing less than a millionaire.

His final dream, to see the place of state government move to Harrisburg, was not realized before his death. But in October 1812, that dream too would become a reality. While he lay in his grave in the churchyard of Paxton Presbyterian Church, the state Assembly voted to move to Harrisburg in an effort to make the state government more central and responsive to the needs of the entire state of Pennsylvania. New York had moved to Albany and Virginia had moved its seat of state government to Richmond. It was time for Pennsylvania to follow suit. With land donated by Harris Jr. and additional land purchased from William McClay, the legislature moved to Harrisburg, meeting in the courthouse until the capital building was finished in 1821.

AFTERWORD

While I believe I know John Harris Jr. very well through this study and interpreting his life, I also know that he was a person from the past. There remains much that I do not know or understand about him. He witnessed things I will never see in my lifetime. He lived through ordeals of the sort that most of us will never experience. He did things that were left unrecorded as he lived out his everyday life—like we all do. We are left to assume much and to piece together a picture of his life like a vast, two-thousand-piece puzzle with pieces missing. We see the general picture, but we do not see the whole with clarity. I wish we did. If I had a time machine, yes, I would visit this man whom I have come to admire, respect, value, appreciate, and revere.

As I bring this to a close, let me offer this thought. Let us remember those who have gone before us and who have given so much, most of which is unrecorded. They lived each day in an effort to make a life for their families and many times, to better their communities. They are the unsung heroes of America's great history. Let us hold on to their memories so that they will never die, but instead live on in our collective memories. This is my hope in writing this work: may all of us remember those who have shaped our lives by investing and giving their lives before us. History is often seen as a dry bit of dates and facts, names and wars, places and events. This book has brought a glimpse into the past and lifted one life to a prominent place. John Harris Jr. was more than just facts and dates. He was a real, live, breathing person who lived like we do today...one day at a time, with hopes and dreams, troubles and challenges, family and love. I raise a glass to John Harris Jr. May his memory live on past the moment you finish these last words. And may you be blessed to know just one of those whose shoulders we stand on today.

ACKNOWLEDGMENTS

One of things I've discovered when researching a person like this...you're never finished. My research has most recently taken me to the Lancaster County Historical Society Research Center and the Historical Society of Pennsylvania. I want to thank the people who tirelessly work at these organizations and who honestly got as excited as I did when we discovered something new. I also want to thank my wife, Julie, who was, on many occasions, my research assistant and my chief editor.

A special thank you to my family, who fully supported me in untold ways. I thank the Historical Society of Dauphin County, whose assistance and encouragement helped bring this book to print. And to the many friends who, like me, are history nerds (you know who you are) and told me that I needed to write this book...thank you! It is my hope that as I peel back the life of this fascinating man, you learn to admire, respect, and maybe even love him as I have come to do over the past years of portraying John Harris Jr., the founder of Dauphin County and of Harrisburg, Pennsylvania.

Supporters
A special thank-you goes out to those who not only supported me as friends and fellow history nerds but also provided much-needed

financial support at the very beginning of the project:
Jeb and Robin Stewart
Doug and Nadine Neidich
Russ and Andrea Faber
Todd and Linda Milano

AUTHOR BIOGRAPHY

The author in character as John Harris Jr.

I have been a lover of colonial history for over forty years and a colonial period reenactor for more than twenty years. I am an active member of the Donegal Township Riflemen, a member of the Continental Line of Revolutionary War reenactors, and the First-Person Interpreters of the ALHFAM (Association of Living History, Farm and Agricultural Museums). I have been an extra in several historical documentaries, such as PBS's *Liberty*, The History Channel's *The American Revolution*, WITF television's *Nine Months in York Town*, and HBO's *John Adams*. I've also had parts in *Pursuit of Honor: The Rise of George Washington* by Paladin Communications and The American Experience production of *John and Abigail Adams,* and I play John Hancock in the visitor center film at the National Constitution Center in Philadelphia.

Just over fifteen years ago, I took on the task of being the first-person interpreter of John Harris Jr., the official founder of the city of Harrisburg and of Dauphin County, Pennsylvania. Harris Jr. was a pivotal character in the life of the colony and the state of Pennsylvania. It's been an honor to portray his life in a wide variety of venues.

Professionally, I am a pastor, currently serving at CrossPoint Church in Harrisburg, Pennsylvania. I serve as president of the Historical Society of Dauphin County and co-chair of the mid-Atlantic region of ALHFAM. I've been married to Julie since 1982, when we honeymooned in Colonial Williamsburg. We currently live in Harrisburg. We have three adult children and two grandchildren. I love colonial history, and I absolutely love spending time with and riding my horse, Dexter—he's a dream come true and has taught me what life must have been like from the back of a horse when that was the only means of transportation.

BIBLIOGRAPHY

"Birth of the Commonwealth of Pennsylvania." Proceedings of the Provincial Conference of Committees of the Province of Pennsylvania. Philadelphia: W & T Bradford,1776.https://www.ushistory.org/pennsylvania/birth3.html.

"Dauphin County Pennsylvania in the Revolutionary War." *New Horizons Genealogy*. http://www.newhorizonsgenealogicalservices.com/pennsylvania-genealogy/dauphin-county/dauphin_county_pennsylvania_in_the_revolutionary_war.htm.

"Letter from John Harris to Col Burd at Ft Augusta, Nov. 20, 1763." Colonial Records of Pennsylvania, Harrisburg: the State of Pennsylvania, 1838. https://archive.org/details/colonialrecordsov5harr/page/753/mode/1up.

"Pennsylvania Assembly: Reply to the Governor, 31 May 1753." *Founders Online* National Archives, https://founders.archives.gov/documents/Franklin/01-04-02-0180. [Original source: *The Papers of Benjamin Franklin*, vol. 4, *July 1, 1750, through June 30, 1753*, ed. Leonard W. Labaree. New Haven: Yale University Press, 1961, pp. 500–502.]

Armor, Wm. C. *The John Harris Mansion, 1766-1897*. Harrisburg, Pennsylvania: Harrisburg Publishing Company, 1897.

Brother Onas, August 27, 1762. *Colonial Records of Pennsylvania*, vol. 8. https://archive.org/details/colonialrecordsov5harr/page/753/mode/1up. Harrisburg: the State of Pennsylvania, 1838.

Brown, Carlyle C. "History of John Harris Founder of Harrisburg, PA." Research compiled in 1971. https://www.angelfire.com/on/Canadiangenealogy/harris.html.

Carmer, Carl Lamson. *The Susquehanna*. New York: Rinehart, 1955.

Commemorative Biographical Encyclopedia of Dauphin County, Pennsylvania. Chapter 7, "The Family of the Founder of Harrisburg." Chambersburg, Pennsylvania: J.M. Runk & Co., 1896.

Egle, William Henry, ed. *Notes and Queries, Historical and Genealogical, Chiefly Related to Interior Pennsylvania*. Harrisburg, Pennsylvania: Pennsylvania State Library, 1932. https://archive.org/details/notesquerieshist00penn/mode/1up?view=theater.

Inglewood, Marian. "*Then and Now in Harrisburg*. Harrisburg." https://www.ancestry.com/search/collections/14086/. [Original source: Inglewood, Marian, Then and Now in Harrisburg. Harrisburg, Pennsylvania: unknown, 1925].

Kelker, Luther Reily. *History of Dauphin County, Pennsylvania*, vol. 2. New York and Chicago: The Lewis Publishing Company, 1907.

Mc McIntosh, Harris. *A Chronicle of the Harris and McIntosh Families*. Compiled in 1980.

Morgan, George H. *Centennial: The Settlement, Formation, and Progress of Dauphin County, Pennsylvania, from 1785–1876*. Harrisburg, Pennsylvania: Telegraph Steam Book and Job Printing House, 1877.

www.ingramcontent.com/pod-product-compliance
Lightning Source LLC
Chambersburg PA
CBHW071014120626
46546CB00003B/1085